The Active Classroom

This book is dedicated to the best teacher I know—my wife, Candy.

The Active Classroom

Practical Strategies for Involving Students in the Learning Process

Ron Nash

CORWIN PRESS
A SAGE Company

For information:

Corwin Press
A SAGE Company
2455 Teller Road
Thousand Oaks, California 91320
www.corwinpress.com

SAGE Ltd.
1 Oliver's Yard
55 City Road
London, EC1Y 1SP
United Kingdom

SAGE India Pvt. Ltd.
B 1/I 1 Mohan Cooperative
Industrial Area
Mathura Road, New Delhi 110 044
India

SAGE Asia-Pacific Pte. Ltd.
33 Pekin Street #02-01
Far East Square
Singapore 048763

Printed in the United States of America

Library of Congress Cataloging-in-Publication Data

Nash, Ron, 1949–
   The active classroom : practical strategies for involving students in the learning process / Ron Nash.
      p. cm.
   Includes bibliographical references and index.
   ISBN 978-1-4129-6086-1 (cloth)—ISBN 978-1-4129-6087-8 (pbk.)
   1. Active learning.   2. Learning strategies.   I. Title.
   LB1027.23.N37 2009
   371.39—dc22   2008006266

This book is printed on acid-free paper.

08   09   10   11   10   9   8   7   6   5   4   3   2   1

Acquisitions Editor:	Hudson Perigo
Editorial Assistant:	Lesley Blake
Production Editor:	Appingo Publishing Services
Cover Designer:	Karine Hovsepian
Graphic Designer:	Sandra Sauvajot

Contents

Foreword

How can I use these ideas in my classroom tomorrow?

This is the fundamental question every teacher asks when given new ideas about teaching, learning, or effectively managing a classroom. Whether attending a staff development session, reviewing a new district-wide initiative, attempting to implement a national policy, or reading a new book on teaching like this one, this is the essential through-line of their thinking. In what way is this information of value to me and my students? How can I apply these new ideas? In the end, for classroom teachers, how these new ideas can change their classroom for the better is the ultimate question.

In *The Active Classroom*, Ron Nash concentrates on answering this question. With just enough theory to ground his approach in brain science, he offers some very clear, practical, manageable strategies teachers can implement the very next time they see their students. Maintaining a wonderful balance between philosophy and practice, the primary focus of the book is what to *do* with the ideas it presents: how to adapt and apply them to any content and for students of all ages.

This is a wonderfully refreshing change from more theoretical books. Of course, educational research can be helpful at pointing our vision toward the most significant educational issues of our times. It can isolate strategic policies or provide goals and direction for a specified curriculum, a grade level, a school, or a nation. Indeed, in the last thirty years, brain research has opened our educational eyes regarding the effects of stress and emotions, food and drink, socialization and isolation, and many other aspects of the learning process on the human brain. The bank of knowledge we are building through research is fascinating and thought-provoking to anyone involved in education. But real classroom teachers, working with real students, still want to know . . .

How can I use these ideas in my classroom tomorrow?

When I was studying for my PhD in Educational Psychology, I was delighted to be deeply immersed in current literature regarding many aspects of learning theory. It was fascinating to read a plethora of current studies being conducted on how to manage a dynamic classroom, and how to facilitate effective learning. Yet—most likely because of my background as a classroom teacher—I found myself continually asking my professors how to use these theories in the classroom.

One of the wonderful things about *The Active Classroom* is that you don't have to read far before that vital, practical piece of the puzzle falls into place. In fact, just by dipping into the book, teachers will be able to begin implementing Ron Nash's ideas immediately. This makes the book a highly valuable resource for busy teachers, who can look at almost any section and within a few minutes select an idea, a tool, or a strategy, and put it into action the next day.

Perhaps even more importantly, I am convinced that the strategies Ron Nash offers within these pages will WORK—because they align with the needs of *today's classrooms and today's learners*. Digital natives are a new breed of learners. With their brains hardwired to expect constant stimulation, outside the classroom their world is a constant riot of games, music, video content, and interaction. The result, as any current classroom teacher will attest, is that teaching techniques used a mere ten to fifteen years ago do NOT work with these learners. At the most elemental level they need to be engaged, engrossed, and ACTIVE during the learning process. Ron's book shows clearly and simply how this can be accomplished on a public budget in a main-stream classroom.

How can I use these ideas in my classroom tomorrow?

In *The Active Classroom* Ron Nash has given us some important answers.

—Rich Allen, PhD

Preface

Years ago, when I was a central office instructional coordinator, I remember a teacher who complained that his students would not sit still and pay attention for a full fifty-five-minute class period. There were two implications close to the surface of that complaint, of course. The first was that if the students would just sit still for any length of time, he could teach them. The second was a tacit request for me to help solve that problem by revealing how he could keep them seated, quiet, and attentive. Frankly, I can't remember what advice I gave, but I know what advice I would give today. I would tell him to quit fighting his students' inclination to get up, move, and socialize; instead, provide a classroom structure *inside which* those students could get up, move, and socialize frequently and productively.

I must admit that, early in my teaching career, my own classroom was a very teacher-centered place. What I saw when I began teaching, I did not question. For example, I realize now what I did not understand then: a fairly high percentage of the classroom furniture in schools is arranged by the building custodians (Jones, 2007). In my first classroom, student desks were in five rows of six, and the space between rows was wide enough for the standard dust mop. As a new teacher, I accepted that configuration because it was what I had been used to in high school and, for the most part, in college. Happily unaware of any *choices* related to room arrangement or methods of delivering content, I simply left the desks the way they were and adapted my teaching style to the furniture, utilizing most often the content delivery method I knew best and had experienced the most: lecture. Completely in line with Goodlad's findings (2004), I spent most of the time in my classroom in what Goodlad refers to as "talking mode," and my students were relegated to "listening mode" as they sat and took notes (p. 229). They would occasionally respond to one of my questions, but structured and purposeful interaction among my students was rare. For years, I went home far more exhausted than they ever did.

Reflecting on those early years as a teacher, I can truly say that nothing much happened in the way of professional development or mentoring to change how I taught. I blundered along as a novice teacher, unaware that there might be better ways to involve my students to a greater extent in the learning process. Mine was the active role in those days, and my students were relegated (by me) to being passive observers.

I also fell prey to asking my students the very questions I had heard a hundred times during my own days in school at any level; for example, "Does anyone have any questions?" or "Does everyone understand what I just covered during this class period?" Those two less-than-powerful attempts on my part to check for understanding were more often than not greeted with shaking heads or blank looks. I probably thought that meant they understood every word and were ready to forge ahead in the textbook to the next section, chapter, or unit. More likely my students had no questions because I gave them little time in class to process any of the information I had presented in my lecture. Mine was an orderly, traditional, quiet, and passive classroom.

The movement toward brain-compatible learning in the past three decades has made available to teachers a veritable plethora of ideas on how to shift students from passive to *active* mode and how to involve them in their own learning to a much greater extent than lecture or individual seatwork will permit. Any school district that makes professional development a priority *increases the number of choices available for teachers.* This book is meant to make teachers more aware of many of the choices available to them today.

One cornerstone of the active classroom is the notion that students bring with them a great deal of knowledge and life experience from which they can build new understandings by reflecting and processing in structured, active classroom settings. Lipton and Wellman (2001) affirm what can be accomplished when students are exposed to new ideas in a purposeful and structured format: "According to Jean Piaget, learning is a process of disturbing current constructs with new experiences and exposure to novel ideas. These discoveries then need to be assimilated and or accommodated to form new conceptual understandings" (p. 58). This journey on the part of students and their teachers is one of discovery, exploration, and layering new experiences and understandings on the old.

One result of my own educational trek over the past 36 years is an appreciation of the fact that teachers and students reverse those roles often. My greatest experience as a substitute teacher was having a classroom full of special education students teach me how to do something I could not do—add and multiply using a new math program with which I was completely unfamiliar. Those fourth-graders took themselves to a new level of understanding by teaching me, and I once again marveled at how much teachers can learn from students. Those kids experienced the intrinsic motivation that comes from having successfully completed something beyond the ordinary, in this case "teaching the teacher." At times like this we are reminded that education is a two-way street.

Over the past two decades, I have had the good fortune to attend many conferences and seminars taught by people who understand the constructivist notion of taking what learners already know and building upon it to achieve essential understandings. When I was an instructional coordinator, our school division engaged the services of Dr. Laura Lipton to work with our central office coordinators on instructional strategies that involve students in their own learning. That two-day experience opened my eyes (and my mind) to new possibilities, and it has helped me in countless ways over the years as I have worked with teachers, administrators, teacher assistants, substitute teachers, and other participants in seminars and workshops. That seminar was the first of many that showed me how I could help students make the critical shift from passive to active mode.

I now understand what I wish I had understood during my early years as a teacher: *that students must be actively involved in the learning process if their classroom experience is to lead to deeper understandings and the building of new knowledge.* Students (and adults, as I have discovered) need to hear it, touch it, see it, talk it over, grapple with it, confront it, question it, laugh about it, experience it, and reflect on it in a structured format if learning is to have any meaning and permanence. Our job as teachers is to facilitate those discussions and experiences in a purposeful and meaningful way.

This book is intended to help teachers discover ways to structure classrooms where what Kagan (1994) calls simultaneous interaction is king; where music energizes and helps facilitate process; where the kinesthetic and the visual join the auditory to create impact; where the teacher becomes part process-facilitator and part relationship-builder; and where students can't wait to get to class . . . and then get up, get down, get energized, and get to work.

So let's get to work ourselves. The book is divided into ten chapters that, I trust, each follow in a logical sequence.

Chapter 1: Creating the Right Environment

Before students allow themselves to become actively involved in classroom activities, they want to know that it is safe to do so—physically safe, certainly, but emotionally safe as well. Bailey (2001) stresses the need for a classroom environment free of humiliation, sarcasm, and threat. Students who are afraid to share or speak out about something will be reluctant to take part in classroom conversations with fellow students, or with the teacher, for that matter. Group dynamics being what they are, any interaction between a teacher and a student affects the rest of the class. From the first day of school to the last, students are observing how the teacher treats individual students, looking for patterns, and adjusting their own reactions and behaviors accordingly (Grinder, 2000). Paying attention to the dynamics of the group is critical to the creation of a safe climate. Procedures and routines are an important part of that process as well. In this first chapter we will look at ways to create a classroom environment in which healthy interaction can occur.

Chapter 2: Incorporating Structured Conversations

Once students feel perfectly safe within the four walls of the classroom, my experience has been that they will take part in the discourse and simultaneous interaction that is an important part of any collaborative classroom. There is, of course, still a place for lecture in the active classroom. Short periods of lecture that are followed by time for processing that information are essential (Lipton & Wellman, 2000). "Learners need time to make sense of new information and ideas on their own; they also need time to think aloud and exchange thoughts with others" (p. 73). This second chapter will explore strategies for creating an interactive environment where students move toward becoming interdependent learners. This involves seeing a student's proclivity for socializing not as an obstacle, *but as an opportunity*.

Chapter 3: Managing Movement in the Classroom

Anyone who has observed children for any length of time knows that they simply have to move. They invent reasons to get up. A student whose pencil is already sharp may break the point in order to earn a trip to the sharpener. A visit to the restroom, preferably one that is farthest from the classroom, may provide an opportunity for a student to stand, stretch, and walk. According to Jensen (2000a), "As learning institutions incorporate more physical activity and less lecture, all of our students, not just the kinesthetic learners or those lacking social skills, will experience increased intrinsic motivation, improved attitudes, more bonding, and yes, even more brain cells" (p. ix). This chapter will provide ways in which students can stand, stretch, walk, talk, and laugh . . . while the teacher facilitates learning through that movement.

Chapter 4: Using Music to Facilitate Process

I have concluded that using music as part of my workshops and seminars has had perhaps more impact on participants than any other tool or strategy. Allen (2002) says that music, assuming it is handled correctly by the teacher, "can unleash the energy of any class and help guide it in a useful direction" (p. 90). Garmston (1997) puts it this way: "Music affects the emotions, respiratory system, heart rate, brain waves, and overall learning capacity of your audience" (p. 157). This chapter will explore some powerful uses of music in the classroom.

Chapter 5: Presenting With Confidence

In my four years of teacher preparation in college, I had exactly one course—Speech 101—that dealt with what is a critical role for any teacher: that of *presenter*. Considering the importance of this aspect of teaching, teacher preparation programs would do well to include a great deal of instruction on presentation skills. The tools of the trade for teachers and college instructors include voice (volume, tone, and pitch), body language, wait time, appropriate humor, facial expressions, purposeful positioning, timing, pausing, listening, and other ways of positively impacting the learning process. We'll consider these components and more in this chapter.

Chapter 6: Teaching to All Modalities

The active classroom is a veritable hub of activity. Students are active participants in an environment that is created specifically for the effective use of discussion, movement, formal presentations, collaborative groups, visuals, and music. Each of the three VAK predicates—visual, auditory, and kinesthetic—is honored in the active setting. One problem is that teachers who are strong in one modality may favor it in instruction, giving short shrift to the other two. Sprenger (2002) puts her finger on a related problem for those teachers who, like me, are auditory: "The students soon discover your desire to talk and will have you on several different tangents, using valuable class time" (p. 78). This chapter will explore ways to combine all three modalities into purposeful activities in order to provide balance, engage students, and enhance learning.

Chapter 7: Using Visuals and Technology

I find it amazing that if I purchased something electronic yesterday, it is already obsolete. Technological advances in education come thick and fast and assist teachers in myriad ways. Unfortunately, we can be so captivated by what these technological marvels *can* do that we lose sight of what they *can't* do: replace good teaching. Many of us can remember a presenter who revealed a new slide in a PowerPoint presentation and then proceeded to interrupt our own silent reading of the text in that slide by reading it out loud. This is one example of the misuse of technology that can lead to dissonance and confusion. The *overuse* of technology can result in students being bored and restless. This chapter will provide some tips on working with technology and visuals in the classroom so that what should be *supporting* the lesson does not wind up *becoming* the lesson.

Chapter 8: Unlocking Doors With Storytelling

There is something captivating about a good story. Alida Gersie (as cited in Maguire, 1998) notes that "Whenever stories are told, stillness falls. We cease our restless frittering" (p. 4). I must admit to having my share of restless frittering as a classroom participant, but not when a story was being told by a teacher, professor, or another student. Stories can be true or not. They can be short or long. But a tale well told has the capacity to transport us to another place, another time, and engage us in a way that few other things can. Take a good story and add the context of historical events, for example, and the two form a powerful partnership. This chapter will provide strategies for unleashing the power of storytelling.

Chapter 9: Considering the New Reality and Practical Applications

Growing up in the 1950s and 1960s, my expectations were vastly different than those of a child or adolescent of today. I was mesmerized by black and white television where the action was often leisurely and unfolded at a pace perfectly acceptable to a baby boomer like me. By contrast, today's kids are bombarded with TV and movie images that flash before their eyes with the rapidity of a machine gun. Video games that promise action and fast-moving visual images have replaced yesterday's board games that today's kids might consider "bored games." Students must be entertained. Their capacity for sitting still for any length of time has diminished. This chapter will consider, then, what has changed over the years to create a "new reality" that affects how kids learn and how teachers must now plan for success. This chapter will also include lesson plans in all four major subject areas. The lessons will demonstrate how teachers can take a fifty-five-minute period or a ninety-minute block and facilitate movement, conversation, and collaboration while dealing with course content.

Chapter 10: Planning for the Active Classroom

The teacher's key to effective planning for the active classroom is to honor the human tendency to want to *share* with others, *move* hither and yon, *laugh* out loud, *think* individual thoughts, and then *write* them down—all within the kind of safe environment that permits and encourages those tendencies. There are some potential obstacles that can get in the way of success in the active classroom: among them a lack of classroom space devoted to movement and interaction; leadership inconsistencies; breadth versus depth of coverage; an overabundance of lecture and individual seat time; competition versus collaboration; and playing the blame game. In this final chapter we will look at ways to remove obstacles to learning.

Perhaps the role of the teacher best approximates that of the orchestra conductor. The musicians make the music, but the conductor is in a position to influence the flow of the music, affecting, by her actions, the volume, tempo, and timing. She gives feedback when necessary and acknowledges effort constantly. A symphony is the ultimate collaborative effort. Everyone contributes. Everyone has different strengths and varying levels of skill, but in the final analysis, the conductor figures out how to combine it all into a supremely satisfying effort. *It is at once the score, the talent, the practice, the discipline, the commitment, the passion, and the ability of the conductor to multitask and influence process that determines the quality of the performance.*

The active classroom is a place where the teacher effectively influences the flow of process and his students do most of the work. The active classroom is a place where students are frequently encouraged to actively reflect on and process information, skillfully practice the art of communication, purposefully move and share, and continually engage in their own learning. Active classrooms are alternately noisy and quiet places. They are usually colorful places and they are always safe places. *It is at once the lesson, the talent, the practice, the discipline, the commitment, the passion, and the ability of the teacher to multitask and influence process that determines the quality of the learning.*

The purpose of this book is to help teachers energize students and energize themselves in the process. My belief is that learning should be active, contemplative, dynamic, purposeful, spontaneous, safe, constructivist, brain-compatible, engaging, reflective, and *fun* for everyone involved in the process, including the person in the best position to choreograph it all . . . the teacher.

Acknowledgments

If I start naming names, the list will never end and I'll forget someone. So let me thank those among my colleagues and friends who know, because I have informed them, that where I am now in my professional career is in large measure due to their support, advice, and mentorship. To my former colleagues on the Apple Team at Plaza Middle, I owe a particular debt of gratitude for demonstrating that team teaching can be a continuous improvement feast and a great experience for teachers, students, and parents alike. In fact, the Virginia Beach City Public Schools gave me many opportunities to grow professionally throughout my seventeen years in that school division. I thank my friends in the Office of Instructional Services and the Office of Organizational Development for contributing to my vision of the active classroom. At every turn they taught me that anything is possible if you let the eagles fly.

From 1994 to 2007 it was my pleasure to bring to Virginia Beach many national educational speakers and consultants who added their insights to the collective knowledge and skills-development of our teachers and administrators. I never failed to learn from those master presenters and educators, and they convinced me over the years that the active classroom can be a wonderful, engaging, and exciting place.

My career has encompassed teaching (middle and high school), educational sales and sales management, and central office administration. Over those thirty-six years I have been privileged to train and learn from thousands of teachers, administrators, substitute teachers, yearbook advisers, and teacher assistants. I thank those whom I was fortunate enough to serve for being great partners in learning.

Special thanks go to six master teachers who allowed me to share their classroom triumphs: Fred Alarcon, Joe Gentry, Dana Jackson, Emma Jeter, Chuck Kenison, and Cindy Rickert. Thanks to Dianne Kinnison and Brian T. Jones for their wonderful illustrations.

Kathleen Dempsey, Jenny Sue Flannagan, Kathy Galford, Lannah Hughes, and Karen O'Meara did an excellent job of creating five lesson plans that capture the spirit and power of the active classroom, and I thank Karen Boone for assisting me with formatting along the way.

I could never have completed this without the assistance of Hudson Perigo and Lesley Blake at Corwin Press, along with Belinda Thresher and Kerrie Tilney at Appingo.

Finally, I would like to thank my wife, Candy, for readily agreeing to my early retirement from the Virginia Beach Schools so that I could follow my dream of writing, consulting, and presenting.

Additionally, Corwin Press wishes to acknowledge the following peer reviewers for their editorial insight and guidance:

Amy Broemmel
Assistant Professor
Department of Theory and Practice in Teacher Education
University of Tennessee
Knoxville, TN

Karen L. Fernandez
Humanities Facilitator
Denver Public Schools
Denver, CO

Rick Froehbrodt
Elementary Educator
National Board Certified Teacher
San Diego City Schools
San Diego, CA

Patti Hendricks
National Board Certified Teacher
Sunset Ridge Middle School
West Jordan, UT

Jim Hughes
New Teacher Support Specialist
West Contra Costa Unified School District
Richmond, CA

Rachel A. Mederios
ELL Teacher and Program Supervisor
Elementary Education
Meridian, ID

Sandra Rief
Speaker, consultant, and author of
   How to Reach & Teach Children with ADD/ADHD
www.sandrarief.com
San Diego, CA

Sara E. Spruce
Professor of Education
Olivet Nazarene University
Bourbonnais, IL

About the Author

Photo credit: Tom Farley

Ron Nash's professional career in education has included teaching social studies at the middle and high school levels. He also served as an instructional coordinator and organizational development specialist for the Virginia Beach City Public Schools for thirteen years. In that capacity Ron trained thousands of teachers and other school division employees in such varied topics as classroom management, instructional strategies, presentation techniques, relationship building, customer service, and process management. After Ron's retirement from the Virginia Beach City Public Schools in 2007, he founded Ron Nash and Associates, a company dedicated to working with teachers in the area of brain-compatible learning. Originally from Pennsylvania, Ron and his wife, Candy, a French teacher, have lived in Virginia Beach for the past twenty-three years. Ron can be reached through his Web site at www.ronnashandassociates.com.

1

Creating the Right Environment

North Carolina High School Classroom: Entering a high school science classroom, I find it hard to locate the teacher because the room is a buzz of activity as she and her students work together on physics projects. It is a student who greets me at the door, explains what he and the other students are trying to accomplish, shows me his extensive data portfolio, and introduces me to his teacher. The teacher takes a moment to show me the data charts on the wall, along with a great many visual displays created by her students. She explains that a low grade is unacceptable, and students continue to problem-solve and make improvements (with the help of fellow students who understand the material) until the grade goes up. I take a picture for posterity and travel from group to group within the classroom. Some students are standing, and others are seated on stools, but everyone is engaged in the lesson.

Virginia High School Classroom: Working with a group of high school seniors, I meander around the room listening in on conversations taking place at four different locations where the students discuss the questions posted on various charts and record their collective responses. Music serves as a backdrop for their conversations. I observe all four groups in turn and, once all four charts have been visited in sequence by everyone in the room, each group's spokesperson reports out on the charted information. Others in the groups have an opportunity to add to what was recorded and reported. I ask a few questions in order to delve a bit deeper into some of the charted data. When the activity is finished, the students return to their seats to the accompaniment of Respect, *by Aretha Franklin. I ask them what they enjoyed most about the class. These seniors loved collaborating with each other and "being treated like adults." It does not take long for one of them to point out to me (a guest teacher for the ninety-minute block) that they have done a lot of passive observing over their years in school.*

***Virginia Fifth-Grade Classroom:** I enter a fifth-grade classroom from which the student desks have been removed. Tables placed around the perimeter of the classroom open up more space for movement in the room's center. The students sing a divisibility cadence. In fact, music is used all day long to manage process. The Ray Charles tune* Hit the Road Jack *triggers movement as students clean up, pack up, and ponder their "hit the road" checklists. Roy Orbison's* Pretty Woman *means "Line up!" The kids move purposefully over a "letters hopscotch" area on the floor. Physical or mental state change techniques are used every few minutes, and celebrations are frequent. Worksheets have been outlawed. Students make up songs about content material and sing them as loudly as possible. They share, they move, they laugh, they dance . . . and they learn. Their classroom and standardized test scores are unbelievably high and they truly love school.*

***Boston Seminar:** I walk into a room filled with colorful posters and upbeat music, and I sit in a chair. (There are no tables.) No sooner am I seated than the seminar facilitator has us stand, gets us moving, and gets us sharing. This goes on for just short of five days, all to the accompaniment of music of every sort. Brief periods of direct instruction are always followed by opportunities to process the information, helping us to create new understandings. The five days fly by quickly and painlessly . . . and the experience illuminates for me the way I learn and, subsequently, changes the way I teach.*

Above we have four different classroom settings, four completely different lessons, and four different instructors. These (true) classroom tableaus have at least two things in common: The students were active participants in their own learning, and the teacher or seminar leader *facilitated process.* Additionally, in each case the students did eighty percent of the work while the teacher, in a supportive and consultative role, did the remaining twenty.

In the first example of the science classroom, the class mantra was "continuous improvement." This wasn't just a catch phrase, but a way of doing business for those students and their teacher. The portfolio that student showed me contained, among other things, a run chart of his grades over the course of the semester. He knew at every point during the semester exactly how much he had improved. There was a class run chart on the wall that showed progress over time. On occasions when the class average went down, the student explained to me, the whole class *engaged in a discussion* as to what might have caused the decline and what could be done to bring the grade average back up. At times when the grades went up, they discussed why that happened as well. Continuous improvement and collaboration reigned. Movement and conversation were built into the lesson plan. Interdependence was the order of the day, and at the *end* of the day, *the teacher and her students were all tired because they had all been engaged during the course of the block.*

Near the end of that high school science class, I had the opportunity to ask some questions of the students as we gathered on stools around one of the black science tables. My first question centered on why they seemed to love this particular class. The answers came quickly and in a torrent, but they all communicated essentially the same thing. Most of their classes, they said, were boring. In most cases they sat passively and listened to the teacher talk for the entire class period; students falling asleep in class was not an uncommon occurrence. *But in that science class they were involved.* The teacher's role (and those students understood her role completely) was to provide a classroom structure that engaged them in their own learning.

She had created an environment where the students could think out loud, collaborate on a regular basis, and make mistakes without fear of being ridiculed by anyone. The students had helped create the class rules at the beginning of the year, and it was apparent that they both understood and followed them. Entering the classroom each day, her students shifted from passive to active for a ninety-minute block, *and they liked it.* They were proud of their teacher and proud of their involvement; they knew the teacher valued them, their opinions, and their progress.

Too often, student thinking is not valued (Brooks & Brooks, 1999).

> When asking students questions, most teachers seek not to enable students to think through intricate issues, but to discover whether students know the 'right' answers. Consequently, students quickly learn not to raise their hands in response to a teacher's question unless they are confident they already know the sought-after response. (p. 7)

What we may characterize as "teacher talk" dominates many classrooms and, according to Brooks and Brooks, "In a flowchart of classroom communication, most of the arrows point to or away from the teacher. Student-initiated questions and student-to-student inter-actions are atypical" (p. 6). Yet we know that "[r]egardless of the topic or task, small-group discussion reinforces classroom learning, assists the brain in recalling the information, and allows students to solve problems collaboratively and explore topics in depth" (Alexopoulou & Driver, 1996, in Tate, 2003, p. 2).

In addition to the complaint that they can't keep their students quiet, secondary teachers often complain (as I once did) that they can't get their students to sit still for long periods of time. There is a reason for this. Students have a basic need to *move*! Sitting still for a fifty-five-minute class period or a ninety-minute block would be tough for most *adults*. Our job as teachers is to provide a structure within which movement can be *channeled*, not suppressed. In plan-ning lessons, teachers need to take into account the VAK Predicates: visual, auditory, and kinesthetic. As learners we possess all these to varying degrees, but our classrooms (particularly secondary) are often geared toward the first two and may ignore the third. Speaking of those who are kinesthetic learners, Sprenger (2002) laments that "[r]ows of chairs, sitting still, and being quiet do not allow these stu-dents' brains to become activated" (p. 77).

Meeting with those high school science students convinced me of the efficacy of the active classroom. The students liked it because they were immersed in a student-centered environment diametrically opposed to the teacher-centered environments they disliked and would have avoided had they a choice. College students with whom I talk tell much the same story. They dislike lecture when it is the sole method of delivery and appreciate being involved in their own learn-ing in an active manner.

So we seem to be left with a clear mandate (if we listen to the research and the students). We need to create classroom environ-ments where *discussion* between and among students is the norm, where the students' need for *movement* is honored, and where the teacher's role is to *build relationships* and *manage process* in a climate conducive to interaction and learning.

The active classroom can be a wonderful place, but it does not *just happen*. In fact, it will not happen at all unless the teacher does what is necessary for students to feel comfortable with collaborative activ-ities that include discussion and movement. A great deal of prepara-tion is necessary if students are to feel safe sharing their thoughts, opinions, and ideas. Establishing procedures and routines, researching structures for communication, providing consistently high expectations, approaching discipline issues with the right mindset, providing clear instructions and directions, and building rapport and trust are all necessary in order to make it possible for effective and meaningful interaction to occur.

Procedures and Routines

The high school science class and the fifth-grade classroom I described at the beginning of this chapter shared two additional important characteristics, and it did not take me long in either case to conclude this through observation. First, well-established procedures and routines were in evidence. Second, there were no discipline issues that were apparent during my visits—and both the students and the teachers indicated that discipline problems were virtually non-existent. My own reflective experience over almost four decades in education has taught me that the first helps make the second possible; i.e., in classrooms where process is paramount, half the battle is won and there are *few discipline issues*. Much of the rest of the battle is won by building relationships. In talking to the high school science students that day, it was apparent that their teacher had done just that. The degree of mutual respect and trust was evident in their words and their behavior during the class. When students are actively and happily engaged in their own learning, there is little time and even less motivation for doing the kinds of things that in more passive classrooms would get them into trouble.

According to Wong and Wong (2005), "The number one problem in the classroom is not discipline; it is the lack of procedures and routines" (p. 167). We are not talking about discipline or rules here. We are concerned with process. Wong and Wong provide a useful distinction between discipline and procedures: "**DISCIPLINE** concerns how students *BEHAVE*. **PROCEDURES** concern how things *ARE DONE*" (p. 169). The teacher who incorporates well-established procedures into her teaching will still need rules and consequences, but will have to refer to them or use them far less often.

In preparing for the school year, then, teachers must become process-oriented and think backwards from the vision. If a teacher envisions an active classroom in which students are purposefully engaged in structured discussion and movement, then she must consider what processes will effectively and smoothly facilitate that vision.

Here are some procedure-related questions that will impact the interactive classroom and need to be answered before the semester begins:

What will be the classroom procedure for:

- getting the students' attention when they are talking or working on an activity and it is time to bring them back?
- communicating with a substitute teacher in advance (when that is possible) so that things run smoothly while you are absent?
- sharpening a pencil?
- assigning homework?
- handing in homework?
- providing students with feedback?
- establishing discussion pairs or groups?
- recording information or data on a chart or on the board?
- collecting (and distributing) assignments or materials?
- leaving to go to the restroom during class?
- class dismissal? (My students learned to ignore the bell and wait for my signal.)
- dealing with students who show disrespect for each other or for the teacher?
- asking a question of them? (How much wait time will you provide?)
- answering a student's question? (Again, how much wait time will you provide?)
- straightening and cleaning the room (*them*, not you) at the end of the class period or school day?
- dealing with emergencies (lockdowns, fire drills, etc.)?

None of these questions relate directly to subject-area content. They are *process* questions, but if they (and others) are not answered, any classroom can become a shambles. Smith (2004) likens procedures to railroad tracks, with content as the train. If the track is laid well, the train will run smoothly (p. 82). Some of the questions in the above list may seem trivial, but any veteran teacher will tell you not one is unimportant. Taking the time to decide exactly what those procedures will be is certain to pay dividends later on in the school year.

Not only should the teacher *establish* procedures, but, according to Wong and Wong (2005), they must be practiced so that they become routine. Their three-step process involves first explaining the procedure, then rehearsing it, and finally reinforcing it with appropriate praise or, if it is not done correctly or quickly enough, rehearsing it again *until it becomes routine* (pp. 174–176). One reason this is so important is that students have many other teachers who have their own unique classroom procedures. If a student goes home at the end of the first day of school with six or seven sets of procedures competing for a place in his long-term memory, the second day is bound to bring confusion as he tries to remember which teachers require what procedures.

Unless the routines are well-established in a classroom, students will find it difficult to make the right choice every time. It is understandable that, left to their own devices or in the absence of clear, practiced procedures; students can—and will—get into trouble. Combine students who are in a passive mode for too long with the absence of established and practiced procedures, and even the most innocent act can lead to difficulty.

As an example, let us consider the pencil sharpener. A wonderful invention, to be sure, and still necessary today despite a spate of laptops. The seemingly innocuous pencil sharpener can be a flashpoint for a very good reason. Let me illustrate with a story that may strike a chord with middle or high school teachers.

> *Picture young Eddie sitting quietly in his seat near the classroom windows. His notebook is open, and his pencil is in his hand, but his mind wanders. He has been sitting listening to a lecture on something or other for perhaps twenty minutes. Eddie is restless and bored. Moreover, he knows there is a full half-hour left in the class period...and then his eyes make contact with the pencil sharpener, a legitimate destination for a student if ever there was one. Eddie's frontal lobe begins to function again as he works out the approximate distance and the available routes. He is not aware of any official policy for sharpening the pencil in this classroom, but a trip to the pencil sharpener certainly seems justified, since his pencil is dull and taking notes is, he reasons, important. Others, on occasion, have made the trip without comment from the teacher, although he can remember the teacher stopping once and staring pointedly at Marty all the way to the sharpener. Might get the stare, then, but a definite plus for the trip is that the route he has mapped out will take him past Betsy. It also takes him past his archenemy, Tony, but passing Betsy in the process makes it worth throwing the dice. He gets up, heads for the sharpener, gets tripped by Tony, falls over Betsy's desk . . . well, you get the idea.*

Suffice to say, then, that the consequences for not establishing, explaining, rehearsing, and reinforcing basic procedures can interfere with or effectively prevent the smooth functioning of the classroom, active or otherwise. The active classroom has at least *one powerful advantage* for anyone who has Eddie and a pencil sharpener in the same room. Eddie's original reason for going to the pencil sharpener had nothing whatsoever to do with his pencil, his notes, or the lecture. He had been sitting for twenty minutes, and he needed to move. His brain's cortex went to work not on the lecture content, but on *how he could get up and* GO *somewhere*. The pencil sharpener just happened to come into his line of sight.

In an active classroom, Eddie would not have found himself sitting still for twenty minutes. He would have been up, moving around, and sharing with someone (maybe even Betsy) a good deal sooner. As we will see in Chapter 4, music might have been playing in the background as he moved to meet with a partner or a small group. The whole trip to the pencil sharpener and its consequences amounted to a symptom of two larger problems: *the lack of established, practiced, and completely familiar procedures and routines, and too much seat time.*

Building Relationships

Another important component of an active classroom is the existence of strong rapport between the teacher and the students, along with effective working relationships among the students in the class. There is a tendency today, given the pressure of high-stakes testing, for teachers to want to begin teaching content on the first day of school. The opportunity cost of that approach becomes apparent later in the year, when the lack of attention to up-front relationship-building results in student misbehavior, at which point the teacher begins to look for ways to "control" the behavior. Bluestein (1999) reminds us that "working to build a positive classroom climate—even if temporarily at the expense of the curriculum—can help us avoid being sabotaged by negative attitudes, weak learning behaviors and unrealistic self-expectations as well" (p. 35).

Rogers & Renard (1999) affirm that "[s]tudents are motivated when they believe that teachers treat them like people and care about them personally and educationally. [Teachers need to] foster relationships that help students see teachers as teachers and not as dictators, judges, juries, or enemies" (p. 34). Having worked with over 50,000 students in the U.S., the Netherlands, and Australia over a fifteen-year period, Wubbels, Levy, and Brekelmans (1997) came to the conclusion that "relationship-building is a prerequisite to a positive classroom climate. Without this piece of the repertoire, teachers cannot fully develop in their practice" (p. 85). Teachers need to constantly and consistently work at developing relationships with students and their parents from the very beginning of the school year.

I recently heard the story of a new teacher at the first faculty meeting of the year. The principal apparently asked the teachers to call several of their students' parents *per week* for the first several weeks of school. What she *heard* was a mandate to call several parents *each day* for the first several days. When he came to observe her classroom in early October, he commented on the excellent behavior of the students. She admitted that she had misunderstood his original request, but credited a good deal of her success with discipline to the multitude of phone calls she made that first week. She built relationships from day one, and it paid off. She was making dozens of "relationship deposits" early in the year against the day when she might have to make "withdrawals." She no doubt found that making a difficult phone call to a parent in November was made easier by having built a relationship in August or September.

Making large numbers of phone calls early in the year has other benefits as well. In my first year at Plaza Middle in Virginia Beach, I called a great many parents in the week prior to the first day of school. Those students, of course, knew very well I had begun calling parents, and the word got around. A wonderful thing happened. Other students began to ask when I was going to make the call to their homes. They knew, you see, that my calls had been positive and untainted by any previous problems between their former teachers and their parents or guardians. The students were in a hurry to establish a positive relationship with a teacher who seemed eager to get things off on the right foot. Using the week *before the students came back to school* to make those positive contacts with parents paid great dividends during the year.

By making those positive phone calls, teachers looking forward to the active-classroom experience model the kind of relationship-building they want the students to mimic in order to make discussion and collaboration successful. Attitude is critical in a smooth-running classroom, and modeling is everything. Teachers who demonstrate by their actions that relationship-building is important to them and to the effective operation of the classroom environment have a much better chance of making it all work. This also means letting students see positive relationships between their teachers and others on the school faculty and staff.

Students who observe negative behavior on the part of the teacher can conclude that negative behavior is perfectly acceptable in that teacher's classroom. A teacher who loses her temper consistently should expect students in her classroom to lose theirs. Jones (2007) provides teachers with a maxim that is essential for success in any classroom: "Calm is strength, Upset is weakness" (p. 180).

Any teacher working with students of any age will be faced with conflict that requires problem-solving skills and/or a decision. The teacher who gets upset will downshift from the cortex to the brainstem (Burke, 2008). In the brainstem, problem-solving and decision-making are no longer possible, although the teacher desperately needs to be able to think clearly and act responsibly. According to Jones,

> [w]hen you are calm, you can bring all of your wisdom, experience, and social skill to bear in solving a problem. When you become *upset* and downshift, none of that knowledge or wisdom is available to you. As the saying goes, ***My life is in the hands of any fool who can make me angry.*** (p. 180)

Interaction among students can lead to opportunities for disagreement between partners in a discussion or other collaborative activities. Risking this kind of frequent interaction means that the teacher must model remaining calm and avoid getting upset in the face of conflict. It may mean pausing and breathing deliberately a couple of times before proceeding. The breathing causes the teacher to relax and, according to Bailey (2001), "Conscious, slow deep breathing brings more oxygen to our lungs and our brains for greater clarity, calmness and energy" (p. 40).

In building relationships, one tool that is often misused, yet should not be overlooked, is praise. Todd Whitaker (2004) credits Ben Bissell (1992) with a description of five things that make praise more effective. Praise must be, according to Bissell, authentic, specific, immediate, clean, and private (pp. 46–47). The last descriptor is particularly important in the classroom. Some students do not like public praise and praising someone who likes their accolades delivered in private may be a demotivator. There is a business maxim called the Platinum Rule, which says that we should do to others as they would have done to themselves. This is true of praise. I once had a supervisor who asked us each how we liked being praised, publicly or privately, and *honored our choice at every turn*. All this is important in the functioning of the interactive classroom, since cooperation is critical in the collaborative environment. Praising publicly a student who does not appreciate that may cause him or her to shut down for a long time, maybe for the rest of the year.

Teachers will often give praise in phrases like "Good job!" or "Excellent work!" Praise that is this general is less effective than praise that is specific. According to Costa (2008), "What makes an act 'good' or 'excellent' must be communicated along with the praise. Thereby, the student understands the reason or criteria that make the act acceptable and thus the performance can be repeated" (p. 214). (See Figure 1.1)

Figure 1.1   Examples of Praise: Inappropriate and Appropriate

Example 1—Inappropriate Praise	Example 1—Appropriate Praise
The teacher passes by Tony's desk while students are working and slaps Tony on the back, saying, "Great work on your essay, Tony!"	The teacher crouches next to Tony while students are working and says quietly, "Tony, I just gave you some feedback on the essay you turned in this morning and I noticed that your verb-subject agreement was correct in every paragraph. That is a definite improvement from last week's essay. I thought you might want to know."
In the situation above, the praise is general, and no really helpful feedback is given to Tony. The reason for the praise may remain a mystery forever, or at least until the essay is returned.	In the example above, the teacher gives Tony some specific feedback from the essay. The feedback may be cause for a bit of celebration on Tony's part, and it may ensure that Tony looks for verb-subject agreement in the future.
Example 2—Inappropriate Praise	**Example 2—Appropriate Praise**
The teacher stops class and has everyone applaud Tina because her grade over the last two similar assignments improved one full letter grade. Tina turns red and covers her face with her hands.	While students are working quietly on an in-class assignment, the teacher motions for Tina to come up front, where, very quietly, he informs her of the good news . . . that her grades are steadily improving. He also gives several concrete reasons for her improvement over time.
This is inappropriate if Tina is the kind of person who hates public praise. Before giving praise publicly, a teacher should know that the object of the praise is okay with it.	The praise here is not only private, but specific. It also gives Tina a chance to ask some questions, but quietly and with no chance of anyone overhearing the discussion.

A teacher, then, must be consistently positive and work *ceaselessly* to build positive relationships. As we have seen, this may begin in late summer with parents and should continue throughout the course of the school year with students and parents alike. Additionally, the teacher must show that remaining calm in the face of conflict or frustrating situations is the best way to deal with both. Genuine and unceasing efforts to build rapport will help build trust, an essential ingredient in the interactive classroom.

Avoiding Demotivators

In *What to Do with the Kid Who . . .*, Kay Burke (2008), in a chapter dealing with classroom climate, lists twelve teacher behaviors that can quickly and effectively dismantle trust as it erodes the climate of the classroom. Doing these things would be bad enough in a classroom where students are passive observers, but the effect of many of these in an interactive classroom would be like shouting in an echo chamber. The teacher who asks students to share frequently in pairs or groups is asking for trouble if she models inappropriate behavior herself.

In Figure 1.2, I have listed Burke's "Dirty Dozen" in the left column, and I have indicated in the right column what *I believe* would be the effect of these behaviors on a class where students are expected to talk, move, and collaborate frequently (p. 87).

Figure 1.2   Adaptation of Kay Burke's Dirty Dozen "Demotivators"

Behavior	Effect in the Active Classroom
Sarcasm	Students will not only be hurt by such sarcasm on the part of the teacher, but will use it themselves when they meet in pairs or groups. Sarcasm or humiliation from any source will inhibit the kind of student interaction necessary in the active classroom.
Negative tone of voice	This will not only turn students off, but will encourage their own use of such negativity in their own discussions.
Negative body language	Any teacher who is working with students on presentation skills will, at some point, have a discussion on body language. Telling students to be *careful* of negative body language and then *modeling* precisely that reveals inconsistencies that will undermine the effectiveness of any discussions or group collaboration.
Inconsistency	Teaching one thing and modeling something else is an example of an inconsistency that can lead to trouble. Procedures need to be consistent as well.

Behavior	Effect in the Active Classroom
Favoritism	In a classroom where the teacher may ask students to scribe or perform other procedural duties, calling on the same person all the time will backfire.
Put-downs	Insulting students (intentionally or not) will erode trust and, once again, set the stage for students to do the same thing when they are in pairs or groups.
Outbursts	Even short bursts of temper model inappropriate behavior, and such outbursts serve to make the other students in the room feel unsafe. If the behavior is repeated, the fact that they could be the next recipient of an outburst or tirade may never be far from their minds.
Public Reprimands	If needed, reprimands should be administered in private. The interactive classroom requires students to talk and share frequently. Being humiliated by the teacher will lead to embarrassment that will carry over into the collaborative activities the teacher is working so hard to put in place. It may also be mimicked by students in the class.
Unfairness	As Burke suggests, "Taking away promised privileges; scheduling a surprise test; 'nitpicking' while grading homework or tests; or assigning punitive homework could be construed as 'unfair,'" and the negativism among students is sure to carry over into any of the interactive activities the teacher has planned, with unintended, but predictable, results (p. 91).
Apathy	The teacher in an interactive classroom is in the role of orchestra conductor. Imagine a conductor whose whole demeanor during practice and a performance is apathetic. If the conductor doesn't seem to care, why should the members of the orchestra . . . or the apathetic teacher's students?
Inflexibility	Teachers must be willing to make adjustments in the classroom based on the needs of the students or on changing circumstances that would affect performance if the change or adjustment is not made.
Lack of Humor	Humor is a key ingredient to success in the active classroom. Teachers, as Burke points out, need to be able to laugh at themselves. Being able to do that encourages students who are sharing frequently to do the same. Burke is right on the money when she says that "humorless classes lack energy" (p. 91). I have found that humorless teachers lack energy as well. Teachers do not have to be naturally funny to use humor. Appropriate jokes, funny stories, and self-deprecating humor are all valuable tools.

These demotivators can cause stress levels to rise significantly. Teachers who regularly scold students and use sarcasm, or whose behavior in the classroom is consistently negative, put students in a position where they find it difficult to learn. Sylwester (1995) says that "high cortisol levels can lead to the despair we feel when we've failed" (p. 38). Further, *chronically* high cortisol levels "can lead to the destruction of neurons associated with learning and memory" (p. 38). As Bluestein (2001) points out, students who are continually anxious and stressed-out can be at considerable risk and may choose to simply disengage altogether and finally drop out of school: "Clearly, a stressful school environment interferes with its instructional objectives" (p. 33).

Teachers who are consistently positive and have rid their classrooms of sarcasm, negativity, scolding, threats, and other demotivators will be much more successful in establishing and maintaining a climate conducive to learning.

Safety is of prime concern to students, and not just physical safety. For example, students may not wish to participate in class because they are afraid they do not have the "right answer" they believe the teacher seeks. Part of creating an environment in which students are more likely to willingly participate is letting them know it is perfectly normal and acceptable to "not know all the answers" (Tileston, 2004, p. 30). When she was an elementary teacher, 1999 Virginia Teacher of the Year Linda Koutoufas had a penny jar on her desk to which she regularly contributed when *she* made a mistake. Koutoufas (2007) says she "eventually created a class of risk-takers—students who were not afraid to risk unique and brilliant answers because they knew they would be supported and that, if incorrect, I would take the time to guide them to a correct answer" (p. 117).

I have found that working with students who are not often active participants and allowing them to taste success can set them up to become more engaged and increasingly more successful down the road. A teacher is in a unique position to determine when what a student has written, for example, could be shared with the class to that student's benefit. My suggestion is that when a teacher determines that this is the case, she should first ask the student (quietly) if he would mind sharing it with the entire class. If the student agrees, then have him share at the earliest opportunity as part of a general sharing activity. If the student demurs, tell him that is fine and perhaps he will choose to share later on. Saying, "That is okay; maybe later," lets the student know the teacher will not force him to share, but will continue to ask. If the student *does* share and tastes success, that is one more building block in establishing the active classroom.

Consistent encouragement on the part of the teacher is paramount. Students must know you believe that they can, and will, succeed. In the active classroom, everyone is involved, not just a small and predictable group of regular players. "When you fail to recognize particular students, you can communicate a low level of confidence in their abilities" (Boynton & Boynton, 2005, p. 8). This may mean that teachers have to limit the number of times they call on individuals in class. Grinder (2000) affirms that it is perfectly acceptable *to the rest of the class* for one individual to ask a couple of questions, but "after the same student has asked several questions, the teacher has the class' permission to delay answering the questions" (p. 35). One way of dealing with this situation is to let the student who keeps asking questions—and by so doing, dominate the proceedings—know that there will come a time his or her latest question will be answered, perhaps one-on-one once the class is engaged in something else or after class.

Shifting from passive to active mode, then, involves not inconsiderable risks on the part of students. Before they are willing to participate in the sharing and interpersonal communication that is the life blood of the interactive classroom, kids need to know it is safe for them to do so. It is the job of the teacher to provide that safe environment. Teachers need to be aware of undercurrents of tension or conflict that can distress or hurt children. In the words of Bluestein (2001), "[k]ids need to know that an adult will be there for them, and that we are capable of intervening and supporting them without making things worse. This means learning to listen, pay attention, and take kids seriously in ways that perhaps we never have before" (p. 286).

Creating a plan to help students with very basic social skills may be necessary before students can share with each other effectively and productively. Bosch (2006) suggests that teachers "have students role-play, read books for discussion on social issues and behaviors, or establish a list of positive ways to communicate with one another" (p. 64). Establishing a set of behavioral expectations for pair, group, or class interaction during the first week of school will pay great dividends later in the year, but only if the teacher sees to it that everyone (including herself) lives up to those expectations.

Teachers planning for the upcoming school year and worrying about student misbehavior can take heart from the classrooms described at the beginning of this chapter and from Tate's (2007) observation that any teacher's "best line of defense against behavior problems is that teacher's ability to actively engage students in meaningful and relevant lessons" (p. xiv).

Final Thoughts on Creating the Right Environment

Let's recap for a moment and look at the hypothetical case of a teacher committed to creating an active classroom. During the first weeks of the semester, she has invested heavily in building strong relationships with students and parents alike. Having read Harry and Rosemary Wong's *How to Be an Effective Teacher: The First Days of School* (2005), she has established, explained, rehearsed, and reinforced good procedures until they have become routine. She has worked hard to keep destructive behaviors like sarcasm, negative body language, and public reprimands out of her classroom environment. She has built trust and rapport with students who were initially reluctant to move from a passive to a more active role. By doing all this she has helped her students expand their comfort zones *to the point where pair and group collaboration may be possible*. The signs are positive, and she is eager to get to the content through discussions and group collaboration.

Yet students who may be used to a more passive, traditional environment will need to be moved gently into a highly active format. A middle school teacher recently told me that when she started using music as students entered her classroom, her students initially reacted with comments like, "What *IS* that?" Hearing music play when they entered the classroom was *different* and, for a brief time, took them out of their comfort zone. The teacher let me know she stayed with it, and now they are used to having music played frequently and they are energized by it. She also has few problems with tardiness because their expectation is that the music will be playing when they enter. Teachers can expect "pushback" when attempting to take students from what may be a more traditional and passive mode to a more active one.

The transition to an intensely active environment will require a good deal of preparation and heaps of patience. In Chapter 2 we'll begin to look at what can be done to help students shift from passive to active mode by strengthening their communication skills.

2

Incorporating Structured Conversations

When I worked in the Office of Organizational Development in the Virginia Beach City Public Schools, I had occasion to work on a team that was creating a document for evaluating one of our programs. Near the end of the day, when the team had worked its way through the document and we thought we were about finished, I handed the draft to the one team member who had been busy elsewhere and had arrived maybe an hour before we all went home for the evening. Reconvening the next morning, we brought this (analytical) colleague into the process, and then we brainstormed, charted, and discussed possible changes. His pointed questions, reasoned arguments, and subsequent suggestions made the final evaluation form a great deal better. None of the rest of us had that analytical bent and he saw things we had all missed. The document was better because we took the extra time to discuss, debate, question, and **seek different perspectives.** *We took the time to talk . . . and listen— i.e., we communicated. When communication is par for the course in an organization or in a classroom, good things happen.*

In the global economy of today, employers need employees who can communicate effectively (Bracey, 2006). If communication is indeed a two-way street, employers and employees alike need to make a conscious effort to understand and appreciate the perspectives of others in the organization. In the 21st century, workforce skills include being "able to work comfortably with people from other cultures, solve problems creatively, write and speak well, think in a multidisciplinary way, and evaluate information critically" (Gewertz, 2007, p. 25). Kagan (1994) says that "students of today must learn to communicate and work well with others within the full range of social situations, especially within situations involving fluid social structures, human diversity, and interdependence" (p. 2:6). Teachers and school districts must begin to recognize that so-called "soft skills" are critical when it comes to our students' future.

At Sacramento New Technology High School in California, collaborating with peers and oral communication are part of the curriculum. Skills in these areas must be mastered in addition to traditional academic material (Gewertz, 2007, p. 25). Beverly Nelson (1996) teaches science in a New Jersey high school with students who represent over ninety-nine nationalities. Her biggest challenge is "persuading students of different backgrounds and cultures to work together" (p. 22). To achieve this end, Nelson forms cooperative learning teams and creates new teams periodically. She recognizes that "students cannot be necessarily expected to function as a team" simply because they have been organized in teams (p. 24). Understanding that being able to cooperate effectively is important for her students, *she works hard at helping them acquire the basic skills needed to make teamwork the norm.*

Ignoring more complex interpersonal skills for a moment, just getting kids to make eye contact with adults can be a problem. Lamenting the fact that "kids spend more time looking at the tops of their shoes than in my eyes when we are talking," Sacramento New Tech High Principal Paula M. Hanzel not only works with teachers to encourage eye contact among students; she also believes that "interpersonal skills will prove just as important to her students' futures as writing a great paper" (Gewertz, p. 26).

We as educators at every level from elementary school to college are going to have to work diligently at helping students develop those communications skills. Citing a Nickelodeon (cable TV network) study, Borja (2005) recounts that almost seventy percent of kids between the ages of six and fourteen have television sets in their bedrooms (p. 11). The same study also revealed that fifty percent in that same age range have video game systems in their bedrooms and "watch an average of 23 hours and 3 minutes of television per week, up from 21 hours and 18 minutes in 1992" (p. 11). This newest figure falls just short of a full day of television per week . . . and that is the *average*.

Setting aside any questions about violence on television, or the benefit of what children are watching on television or learning from their video games, one thing seems crystal clear. *While they are watching television or playing video games, they are not developing social skills necessary for success in the active classroom, the workforce, or for life in general.* Like Beverly Nelson above, teachers all across the country need to take the time to help students learn to communicate and collaborate effectively.

If students are indeed spending more and more of their own time in front of two-dimensional screens, then classrooms must become three-dimensional laboratories where students can acquire the skills they need to be successful. Structured conversation is an important part of that equation. Students who are petrified to talk in front of a group can begin to overcome that fear by working in pairs and then in small groups.

First Things First

The learning process can be a lonely exercise. Students often complete worksheets on their own. They are left to ponder alone the meaning of a film they have just seen. Student desks are in rows that discourage conversations with classmates. Often, the conversations that do take place are between the teacher and the few students who process information quickly and are not afraid to speak in front of a room filled with their peers. I spent a good many years as a teacher having conversations with a mere handful of my students in any given class. The others were polite, for the most part, but they were not engaged in any meaningful way. Early in my career, I rarely had students work in pairs or in groups to discuss anything meaningful or to problem-solve. I spent a lot of time saying, "Do your own work, please!"

When teachers do most of the talking and when interactions are between a few students and the teacher, those students *not* involved in the conversation have tacit permission to disengage. Students who are not encouraged to communicate frequently will not, unsurprisingly perhaps, learn to communicate well. Because they are not engaged, they become bored. When students take part in paired or group discussions, they are involved and engaged in their own learning. According to Kagan (1994), when students are paired for conversations, half the class is talking, and when this happens, "There is 15 times as much student language production over subject matter" (p. 4:7). Kagan calls this the simultaneity principle.

Part of the problem with getting students to share, of course, is that speaking in front of a group of their assembled peers frightens many children, even in the best of circumstances. Indeed, I know many adults who can teach all day long and enjoy it, yet are petrified of presenting at a faculty meeting or speaking to a group of parents at a PTA meeting. Much of that fear comes from the possibility that taking the risk of sharing will result in embarrassment. "Fear of physical harm and fear of embarrassment often have the same effect" (Rogers & Renard, 1999, p. 35). Teachers need to create the kind of safe environment in which students are not afraid to open up and risk failure in the form of embarrassment or humiliation.

There also may be anxiety on the part of students as to how the teacher or their peers will react to what they share with the class. If students are unclear about how a teacher or their classmates will respond, they may be less likely to take the risk. According to Burke (2008), "Students do not feel free to engage in interactive discussion, contribute ideas, or share experiences if they are never sure when they will incur the teacher's wrath or become the object of the teacher's sarcasm or anger" (p. 85). If they feel safe, structures for conversation can be put in place on a regular basis. Tate (2003) affirms, "When students are given the opportunity to brainstorm ideas without criticism, to discuss opinions, to debate controversial issues, and to answer questions at all levels of Bloom's taxonomy, wonderful things can happen that naturally improve comprehension and higher order thinking" (p. 1).

Once teachers have created a truly safe climate in which students are willing to share, they can begin to plan for a good deal of structured conversation. In the next chapter we'll look at room arrangements that will facilitate movement in the classroom. Suffice it to say here that in order for students to be able to hold a conversation while seated, student desks may need to be arranged differently. Hanging across an aisle in order to engage in a discussion can be inconvenient at best and can sometimes be downright dangerous. In a traditionally arranged classroom, simply moving the desks a bit closer together to provide each student with a partner is a good start.

A student who may be afraid to communicate orally with the whole class may be willing to share with one other person with whom he feels comfortable. Any teacher who is putting students in pairs for the first time may want to consider carefully who is paired with whom. First things first, and the first thing is to get students talking with someone they know and trust *about something with which they are familiar*. The idea here is to get the *process* down while providing a formal structure to which they can become accustomed over time.

Working in Pairs

Assume for the moment that a teacher has spent a good deal of time at the beginning of the year establishing rapport, building positive relationships, embedding powerful and effective procedures and routines, and in general, establishing a climate in which students will not mind sharing ideas with each other. Realizing that the next step in the transition to an interactive classroom may be providing a structure for students to communicate orally and openly, he must make a decision about how that might be accomplished. My advice to him would be to begin by having students work in pairs.

Early in the year, Burke (2008) recommends that teachers assign each student a partner. For five minutes, the students simply get to know each other, finding out about hobbies, clubs, and other interests. Next, each pair joins *another* pair and, for a total of about eight minutes (two minutes for each student in the quartet), partners introduce each other to the other pair. "This strategy provides a nonthreatening way for students to practice the basic interaction skills of introducing themselves, starting a conversation, smiling, carrying on a conversation, being polite, and using first names" (Burke, 2008, p. 104). Once again, it is critical to allow students to get the whole sharing/discussion process down before introducing subject-area content into the equation. Students simply need to get used to the idea of having conversations with each other frequently in pairs or groups.

There are at least five advantages of beginning the interactive journey with pairs, rather than larger groups of students:

1. A conversation with one other peer may be far less threatening than speaking in front of the whole class, especially if there is music playing in the background to make the conversation more private. (The multiple and purposeful uses of music will be discussed in Chapter 4.)

2. In a pair there is no place to hide. My experience has shown that, in a very large percentage of cases when students share in pairs, both partners contribute *something* to a given discussion. One partner may dominate, but we will look at ways to eliminate that later on in the book.

3. The classroom can be set up so there is a more-or-less permanent partner for each student. Prior to class, desks can be
   arranged so that the partners can have a conversation on cue,
   problem-solve in pairs, and help each other with difficult
   concepts.

4. With the desks in pairs, it opens up wide pathways for the
   teacher (and students) to move about freely.

5. Students who learn to work effectively and safely with a single
   partner will be less likely to resist the next step—the move to
   collaborative groups.

Let's take a look at a simple activity that might help students
make the transition from a traditional classroom setting (straight
rows, students working alone) to a more dynamic setting where students begin to communicate about a familiar topic. While the student
practices the art of oral communication, the teacher practices managing process. The purpose of the activity is to establish a baseline, if
you will, for effective pairing in the classroom. Each time the process
is repeated within the established and increasingly familiar structure,
the teacher and her students will become more proficient. Once the
process has been honed, *subject-area content* can be introduced. Figure
2.1 lists some possible topics for paired conversations.

Figure 2.1 Possible Topics for Discussion When Students *First* Work in Pairs

First level (little thought required):	Next level (more thought required):
Their favorite… • Television shows • Movies • Books • Heroes • Vacation destinations • Cartoon characters • Food • Candy • Sports • Outdoor activities	• Ways to build respect when working with other students or family members on a project • Favorite places and techniques to study for tests • Ways to stay healthy and live a long life • Considerations families may have when deciding whether or not to move to another house, city, state, or country

As part of the process for any classroom conversation, the teacher
will need a way to bring the students' attention back to her when she

is ready to end the discussion. I use a signal that combines the visual and the auditory, no matter the age group. I hold my hand in the air and say, "Pause; look this way please. Finish your thought, but not your paragraph." I explain that while I don't want the participants to cut off their discussion in mid-syllable, I don't want them to continue for more than a few seconds. In other words, I want to honor the fact that I asked them to speak by permitting them to finish a thought or sentence before we move to the next activity. I have observed hundreds of teachers, trainers, presenters, and seminar facilitators over the years, and the most successful process managers are those who invest two minutes up front to establish this norm. It is cheap, but it pays great dividends immediately.

TTYPA (Turn to Your Partner and . . .)

Think about the process of lecturing for a moment. A teacher or professor stands up front and imparts information to students who are seated and taking notes. There are at least three things to consider from the vantage point of the student:

1. As the instructor talks, the student attempts simultaneously to listen and take notes without missing anything—no easy task under the best of circumstances. The idea, of course, is that the student will later reflect on the notes and process the information on his own at home, when he is some distance in time and space from the lecture.

2. While grappling with listening and taking notes, something the instructor just said happens to strike a responsive chord in the student's mind. He begins to ponder it while looking out the window. While he processes the information, he suddenly hears the instructor, in a change of pitch or tone, announce *point three*. The student muses, "What happened to *point two*?" The lecture is continuing apace, however, so he looks at someone else's notes to pick up on point two while missing point three . . . and so on throughout what may be a lengthy lecture. There is no rewind button for the student in this situation.

3. All of this presupposes that there are no distractions during the lecture. Students may be arriving or leaving, the temperature may be uncomfortable, something may be going on outside the window, someone may be passing notes, a student

with a cold may be coughing frequently . . . distractions can come in bunches, playing havoc with the whole process.

If we add to all this the fact that the average time an adult can pay attention during a presentation is fifteen minutes or less (and the attention span decreases as the age decreases), then the natural inclination to stop paying attention simply adds to the other difficulties described above (Allen, 2002, p. 31). The message here is that after ten or, at the most, fifteen minutes of lecturing, teachers and other presenters simply need to do something else. That something else can be as simple as saying, "Turn to your partner; take a moment to discuss point number one before moving on to point number two." Or, "Turn to your partner and see if you agree with what the author says on page twenty-two."

Fogarty (1990) gives a convincing reason why TTYPA is so effective. "It is next to impossible to turn to your partner and . . . not say something. This simple strategy has a compelling ingredient in it. There is a built-in expectation for reciprocity. It's hard to drop out of a twosome when your partner is depending on you to complete the interaction" (p. 10).

Giving students some time to process the information the teacher just delivered will help them remember it. Both partners may have received a different message from the same lecture segment. Talking about it may help them understand it a bit better, or cause them to see if from the partner's perspective. As the teacher circulates around the room and listens to the various conversations, she will get an idea of how well they understand that ten minutes' worth of information. If the students seem to be confused as they share, that may be an indication that the teacher needs to go back and work with the information a little more (and maybe from a different angle).

Timed Pair Activity

One way to get structured conversations started is with a short timed conversation, maybe sixty seconds, in which students pair up and then choose a topic for discussion. It could be a topic from the list in Figure 2.1 or something else students choose to discuss. The idea is simply to get them talking while the teacher observes the conversations. Here, step-by-step, is what it might look like:

1. Once students are paired, ask them to share with each other on a topic that interests them. It might be that they each tell a

story related to their own past. Let them talk for about sixty seconds while you circulate around the room.

2. After sixty seconds, or if you notice a significant drop in conversation volume, use whatever norm you established (raising your hand, striking a note on a set of chimes) to bring them back to you. Mentally gauge the amount of time it took to bring them back. If the amount of time it took them to get quiet was acceptable, congratulate them. If the amount of time could be improved, tell them it was good *and* that their goal is to improve over that first time.

3. Now introduce a new topic (again, something with which they are all very familiar), and set them to work discussing it while you circulate around the room.

4. After sixty seconds, or at the point where the volume decreases noticeably, use your signal again and, once more, compare the time it took them to finish. If the wrap-up time was shorter in the second conversation (and my experience has been that it usually is), congratulate them and thank them.

5. Have each student turn to his or her partner and say, "Thanks for sharing."

6. Step outside the activity for a few minutes with the class as you look at process. How do they think it went? Did they each get a chance to talk during the two sixty-second sequences? If not, ask them what you could do as a teacher to help solve that. Someone will most likely suggest a time limit for each partner. When you hear that suggestion, stop and get them ready to go one more time with a different topic and a time limit of thirty seconds for each paired partner.

7. This time around, ask them to decide who will be Partner A and who will be Partner B. Have those who chose A raise their hands. Do the same for the Bs in the room. Tell them that B stands for Begin, so B will speak first.

8. Again, pick a topic with which they are familiar and comfortable (e.g., What are their plans for the future?). Announce that you will say "Switch!" when it is time for A to pick up the conversation. Look at your watch so they know you are going to follow through with the timing process, and say, "B, tell A about what you want to do when you graduate, and tell him what you think you need to do to get there or do that. GO!"

9. Give B thirty seconds and say, "Switch!" Give A thirty seconds, and use your signal to get them to wrap it up and look at you. Ask them if the second way (timed) was better than the first. Ask them, "What does switching from B to A or A to B guarantee?" Students should note that, in this way, each student gets a chance to share, and for the same amount of time.

This entire activity should take no more than about twenty to twenty-five minutes, including the initial instructions and the debriefing in the middle and at the end. The key to its effectiveness as an activity is the comfort level of the students with the process itself. Once the process has been internalized and students have tasted some success in this basic collaborative activity, the teacher can introduce subject-area content into the mix.

The teacher is in constant motion during this collaborative exercise. Her job is to keep track of the time and to listen in on various conversations with an eye toward accomplishing two things. First, listening in to content-area discussions will give her a chance to determine whether the discussions are going as she intended. By moving around and listening carefully, she can determine whether students are indeed on task (and not discussing the Friday night football game), and she can ascertain whether the information they are sharing in the conversations is accurate. If she overhears some consistent and widespread factual errors, she can, when they are finished, take the time to go over that particular concept or topic once more in order to correct some misconceptions and incorrect information. The entire exercise becomes a two-minute formative assessment tool and gives the teacher information that will help her make a mid-course correction, if necessary, before proceeding to new material.

The second reason for listening in on various conversations is to spend some time near a couple of students who normally do not share in class. If in the discussions involving those two students there is something that is share-worthy, the teacher can ask the partners whether they would share those thoughts with the entire class during the debrief. If they say yes, she can call on them later to share what they said during their conversation. If they are reluctant to share with the class themselves, she can ask if it would be permissible for her to share it and give them credit. One way or another, they contribute to the overall discussion and end-of-activity summarization in a way that they may not have done before. Success breeds confidence, and confidence may lead to a greater role for those students in future discussions and collaborative activities. Remember, these are not students who would normally share their thoughts in front of the entire group, but this structure provides them with an opportunity to make some progress on the communication front.

Any paired activity should always end with an instruction from the teacher for each partner to acknowledge and thank the other (a *gentle* high-five might be appropriate), followed by the teacher complimenting the class on how things went. Here, I suggest that teachers *get specific with any praise*. Instead of saying something that adds up to "nice job," she might say, "I noticed during this conversation that you seemed to have a good grasp of the sequence of events during 1863. In your conversations, most of you mentioned the Emancipation Proclamation in January and the Battle of Gettysburg in July. These are two critically important Civil War events, and you brought them out in your conversations." If she then tacks "Nice job!" or "Well done!" onto the end of *that* closing thought, it means something.

The bottom line here is that *the teacher is providing a structure for simple conversation*: practicing initially with non-threatening, personal discussion topics until the process has been internalized, and then taking an active part in the activity by listening and observing how and what students are doing.

There is one other intended consequence of simultaneous interaction strategies such as the one outlined above. The work load transfers from the teacher to the students. Students move into an active, rather than passive, mode. Every student is involved in the discussion. The teacher shifts to the important role of process facilitator: at times listening, monitoring, encouraging, timekeeping, and always in motion.

Brainstorm and Pass

Brainstorming is a time-honored way of generating lots of ideas for solving a problem or for soliciting feedback relative to a proposed course of action. The problem with brainstorming in the way it is usually used is that only a few students in a class of twenty-five may actually contribute. The teacher may get a recorded or charted list of some sort, but the items on the list came from, in all likelihood, the "usual suspects." My experience is that most of the work is done by the teacher, commenting on the information received while he or she charts the resulting ideas. As in the previous pairing activity, we may want to shift the work load to the students in another interactive exercise where the teacher once again shifts to the role of process facilitator.

Brainstorm and Pass (Lipton & Wellman, 2000) is a structure that not only moves students into an active mode, it ensures that everyone is able to contribute. Regardless of the ideas being generated, each member of the team has the opportunity to add something or pass—meaning, they don't have anything to contribute at this time. A list of generated ideas can be made by a recorder on the team whose job it is to capture the ideas, *regardless of how that person or anyone else in the group feels about the idea.* Debate or an acrimonious discussion at this point will derail the process. The purpose of brainstorming in this fashion is to capture the ideas of everyone in a small group.

Once the students have captured the ideas and recorded them, the teacher instructs each group to choose a reporter (anyone except the recorder). The teacher can then chart a master list of ideas (or have someone else do it) as each reporter reads one item at a time from his or her list, crossing out those items that have been charted already. Once the lists are exhausted, the teacher can then have the class cluster the items into categories for ease of discussion. My experience over the years is that using Brainstorm and Pass provides much more data than the traditional method of simply asking the whole class for ideas or information.

Final Thoughts on Incorporating Structured Conversations

Structured conversations provide students with an opportunity to process information and develop communication skills. There are many strategies for students to share while seated. Furniture can be arranged to facilitate discussions between two students or among groups of students. The next chapter introduces movement into the equation. Blaydes Madigan (2004) informs us that "About 85% of school age children are natural kinesthetic learners" (p. 20). Chapter 3 demonstrates ways to get students up and moving, adding the kinesthetic to the auditory learning modality.

3

Managing Movement in the Classroom

In my years of teaching and observing other teachers, one thing is clear: Students seem to spend a good deal of time thinking of ways to get up from their seats and move around the room or into the hallways. A trip to the pencil sharpener becomes a necessity for a student whose pencil is probably sharp enough. A few minutes in the hall becomes the goal of a student who may not really need to go to the restroom. The trip itself is the real motivator, because the alternative is to sit still for yet another extended period of time. Teachers who fight that natural impulse are missing a great opportunity to harness this natural proclivity for movement.

One of the basic tenets of brain-based learning is that movement facilitates the learning process (Blaydes Madigan, 2004; Dennison & Dennison, 1994; Sprenger, 2002; Wolfe, 2001). Jensen (2005a) makes the case that "movement can be an effective cognitive strategy to (1) strengthen learning, (2) improve memory and retrieval, and (3) enhance learner motivation and morale" (p. 60). Erlauer (2003) puts it this way: "Students who are required to stand or move around during a lesson have less physical fatigue and therefore concentrate more efficiently on the concepts or tasks at hand" (p. 46).

My experience working with adults over the past twelve years is that the same principle applies to them. Adults can't sit for long periods of time without their eyes glazing over and their minds wandering. Teachers working with students and workshop facilitators working with adults would do well to provide plenty of opportunities for movement and, while class participants are standing, for structured conversations. One of the accommodations needed to encourage simultaneous conversation and frequent movement has to do with furniture arrangement.

I taught in a dozen different classrooms in my teaching career, and in every one of those classrooms, the teacher's desk was front and center when I arrived. The student desks were in straight rows with everyone facing the front of the room. In every new classroom I left all the furniture that way and discovered that lecture and an overhead projector fit very well into that room arrangement. This arrangement is teacher-centered, not student-centered, and makes the active classroom difficult to achieve.

There are two major problems with that traditional furniture arrangement. One relates to classroom discipline. When the desks are in neat rows and fill most of the room, it is difficult for the teacher to utilize a critical tool in managing students: *proximity*. The room arrangement shown in Figure 3.1 "produces *five impermeable barriers* between the left side of the room and the right side" (Jones, 2007, p. 38). The feet of many students in a crowded classroom may touch the desk in front of them, making movement difficult. A teacher who needs to respond immediately to a problem four or five rows away will almost always have to go completely around the phalanx of desks to get there.

If this room arrangement creates mobility problems for the instructor, it also means that if students are going to move about the room in order to meet and discuss something, they will encounter not only furniture, but each other, as they try to get to the outside perimeters of the classroom. If you then ask them to find a new partner, movement once again will be confined to the perimeter. With a limited amount of space and the student desks filling the entire center of the room, movement becomes problematic. Figure 3.1 shows the typical arrangement found in most secondary classrooms in North America.

To facilitate movement, teachers are advised to get the teacher's desk, typically front and center, out of the way (banishing it to a corner or to the back of the room). This opens up space in the front of the room. Jones

Figure 3.1

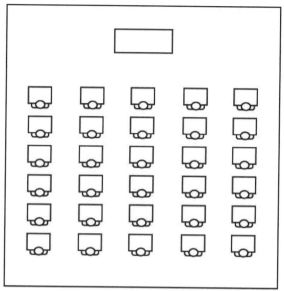

Source: Brian T. Jones, used by permission of Frederic H. Jones & Associates, Inc.

(2007) suggests an arrangement like the one in Figure 3.2, one that contains an "interior loop with ears" to allow the teacher greater freedom of movement. It has the advantage of putting students in pairs to facilitate interaction. In a highly active classroom this configuration gives everyone more space to maneuver and meet during paired or group activities.

Figure 3.2   "Interior Loop With Ears" Room Arrangement

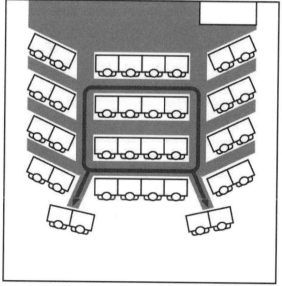

Source: Brian T. Jones, used by permission of Frederic H. Jones & Associates, Inc.

One really effective way to create more space is to move the student desks completely to the outside, opening up the entire center of the room for movement and structured conversations. This perimeter furniture arrangement allows a great deal of flexibility in terms of student and teacher movement.

Figure 3.3   Perimeter Room Arrangement

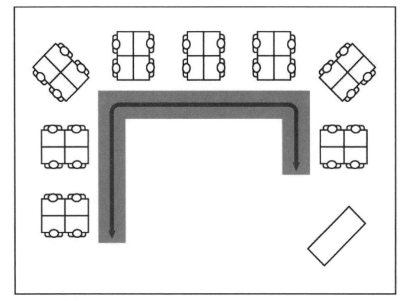

Source: Brian T. Jones.

Take a close look at Figures 3.2 and 3.3. Notice how the students in both configurations are in pairs or in groups of four. Space is created by pushing desks together. Not only does this allow the teacher more mobility; *it also allows students more room in which to meet and process information, and the routes to get to those open spaces are shorter.* The teacher can have students share with the person next to them or with the person across from them; or the *entire group* of four can communicate on some topic on request. In Figure 3.3 the entire center of the room is opened up so students can stand, meet, and move.

If we accept, then, that students need to move and that attending to room arrangement is a necessary and important precursor to that movement, we can explore some suggestions of just how to use that movement to help class or seminar participants process information on their feet. Each of the following strategies involves a structured conversation that allows students to verbalize points of view, summarize information, compare answers, gain new insights, and process new information.

In the last chapter we introduced strategies for conversations or brainstorming with students in their normal classroom seating arrangement. The following strategies ask students to stand and move about the room in order to meet with someone not in their original table group. Meeting with students outside their own closely-knit groups may be uncomfortable, but part of developing communication skills involves moving outside this familiar circle of friends. One high school teacher I know makes it clear from the beginning of the school year that students will meet at one time or another with everyone in the room and not just with their close friends.

Paired Verbal Fluency (PVF)

One of the problems associated with students discussing something in pairs is that one student may dominate the conversation, leaving his partner in the proverbial dust for the amount of time allotted by the teacher for the conversation. The dominant student continues to build his communication skills while his partner is relegated to a minor and not very interesting role in the proceedings. Paired Verbal Fluency (Lipton & Wellman, 2000) ensures that both partners get a chance to share and begins with the establishment of learning partners and a quick decision as to who will be partner A and who will be partner B. The teacher assigns a topic to be discussed and then has A or B go first.

Teachers will want to explain that *attentive listening* involves facing the partner directly, establishing good eye contact, and utilizing positive body language. Over the years, I have worked with middle school students on facilitating groups. The whole concept of making eye contact and paying attention to body language is something I found we had to work on extensively before we could do anything else. If the listener in a pair is partner A and his body language is negative or demonstrates indifference (Figure 3.4), the conversation will never get off the ground.

I found it useful to have students stand with their backs to any wall in the classroom and then concentrate on flattening themselves against the wall. I then instructed them to take one step away from the wall and drop their shoulders. This had the effect of turning their palms in and bringing their heads down to eye level. (Try it!) The relaxation is important. In working with adults on this, I have found that some of them will stand rigidly at attention while facing a partner. This is unnatural and tends to distract the speaker.

Figure 3.5 shows a supportive posture that students can use when they are in the role of listener. Note that the feet are slightly apart. The smile is intended to encourage the listener's partner. Most importantly, there are no distractions for the speaker (smirks, scowls, arm waving, hands in pockets, extravagant gestures, slouching, or sighing). Students have enough difficulty focusing and conversing without the additional obstacles that negative body language and facial expressions can create.

Getting students to adopt a supportive posture like that in Figure 3.5 is only half the battle, however. The student who is in the role of the listener has to, well, *listen*. According to Costa (2008), we often "say we are listening, but in reality we are rehearsing in our head what we are going to say next when our partner is finished" (p. 33). Moreover, according to Costa, "[w]e wish students to hold in abeyance their own values, judgments, opinions, and prejudices in order to listen to and entertain another person's thoughts" (p. 33). This is difficult for students even in the best of circumstances. Keeping one's body language neutral and supportive is difficult, to be sure, but it is necessary if students are going to engage in conversations and process information in pairs or groups. Teachers need to take the time *to talk about and model* supportive listening for students as they work to develop their own conversational skills.

Figure 3.4   Indifferent Posture

Source: Brian T. Jones.

Figure 3.5 Supportive Posture

Source: Brian T. Jones.

As you will see in the step-by-step approach to Paired Verbal Fluency (PVF) in Figures 3.6 and 3.7, it is often necessary for students to summarize what a partner has just said *or* continue a discussion on the same topic without repeating what the partner communicated a minute or so earlier. The listener can't simply mentally disconnect, nod, smile, and go somewhere else in his mind. If Partner A goes first, Partner B must listen carefully because his contribution to the conversation is dependent to a large extent on what A already shared. Partner B will have to summarize or add to what A contributed to the conversation; listening carefully, respectfully, and supportively is therefore essential.

When using PVF, teachers should give one direction at a time whenever possible. Figure 3.6 outlines one possibility for the use of PVF. I strongly encourage that this be done with the students standing up, which is why I included it in the chapter on movement. I have found that if students are standing and facing each other, there are fewer distractions than if students are sitting at their desks. In fact, facing each other from across two typical student desks (and across piles of paper, books, laptops, etc.) can be awkward. Standing in an open area free of clutter allows both students to face each other and share in normal conversational tones. If teachers decide to have them switch partners during the activity, they are already on their feet and can move quickly in order to engage someone else in the class.

Figure 3.6   Paired Verbal Fluency (PVF) as a Step-By-Step Activity, With Directions

Note: Give the directions one at a time.
Direction: "Stand up, and find a partner other than someone at your table."   **Direction:** "Decide who will be **A** and who will be **B**."   **Direction:** "**A**, raise your hand." and "**B**, raise your hand." (then) "Hands down!"   **Direction:** "Our topic for discussion is _____. **A**, when I say GO!, I'll give you 60 seconds to talk about the topic. Now **B**, while **A** is talking, listen carefully. When I say Switch!, **B** will begin talking about this same topic with a twist. You may not repeat anything **A** said during his 60 seconds of fame."   **Direction:** "Look at the board once again to see the topic."   **Direction:** "**A**, you are on . . . GO!"
Partner **A** speaks directly to Partner **B** for 60 seconds on the chosen topic.
Direction: After 60 seconds the teacher says, "Switch!"
On the same topic, Partner **B** takes over for 60 seconds, without repeating what **A** said.
Direction: After 60 seconds the teacher says, "Stop! Look this way."
Direction: "Well done. Thank your partner for sharing. On to the next step."   **Direction:** "This time, **B** will go first. As you think about the 2-minute conversation you and **A** had a few moments ago, were there some things left un-discussed, something important left out? When I say GO!, you'll have 30 seconds to add whatever you think has yet to be discussed as it relates to the topic. When I say Switch!, **A** will have another 30 seconds to add whatever he thinks has not been disclosed about the topic."   **Direction:** "**B**, you are on . . . GO!"
On the same topic, Partner **B** goes first and adds whatever he thinks might have been left out of the initial conversation.
Direction: After 30 seconds the teacher says, "Switch!"
On the same topic, Partner **A** adds information he thinks was left unsaid so far in the conversation.
Direction: After 30 seconds the teacher says, "Stop! Look this way."
Direction: "One final task, and **A** will go first. When I say GO!, **A** will summarize in 20 seconds or so some of the most important points made by both of you during the conversation. When I say Switch!, **B** will have the opportunity to summarize any points not made by **A** in a final 20 seconds. Questions?"   **Direction:** "**A**, you are on . . . GO!"
Partner **A** will summarize what was said so far.
Direction: After 20 seconds the teacher says, "Switch!"
Partner **B** adds to the summary what **A** may have left out.
Direction: After 20 seconds the teacher says, "Stop! Look this way."
Direction: "Thank your partner for sharing, and take your seats!"

Below (Figure 3.7) is another variation, again requiring strong listening and summarization skills on the part of both students. In this case, sixty seconds of conversation on the part of one partner is directly followed by a thirty-second summary by the other. The roles are then reversed for the final phase.

Figure 3.7 A Shorter PVF as a Step-By-Step Activity, With Directions

Note: Give the directions one at a time.
Direction: "Stand up and find a partner other than someone at your table." **Direction:** "Decide who will be **A** and who will be **B**." **Direction:** "**A**, raise your hand." and "**B**, raise your hand." (then) "Hands down!" **Direction:** "Our topic for discussion is _____. **A**, when I say GO!, I'll give you 60 seconds to talk about the topic. Now **B**, while **A** is talking, listen carefully. When I say Switch!, **B** will summarize what **A** said. In order to be able to do that effectively, you must listen carefully while **A** is speaking." **Direction:** "Look at the board once again to see the topic." **Direction:** "**A**, you're on . . . GO!"
Partner **A** speaks directly to Partner **B** for 60 seconds on the chosen topic.
Direction: After 60 seconds the teacher says, "Switch!"
Partner **B** summarizes what **A** said.
Direction: After 30 seconds the teacher says, "Stop! Look this way."
Direction: "Well done. Thank your partner for sharing. On to the next step." **Direction:** "This time, **B** will go first. As you think about the 2-minute conversation you and **A** had a few moments ago, were there some things left un-discussed, something important left out? When I say GO!, you'll have 60 seconds to add whatever you think has yet to be discussed as it relates to the topic. When I say Switch!, **A** will have 30 seconds to summarize what you said." **Direction:** "**B**, you're on . . . GO!"
On the same topic, Partner **B** goes first and adds whatever he thinks might have been left out of the initial conversation.
Direction: After 60 seconds the teacher says, "Switch!"
Partner **A** summarizes what **B** said.
Direction: After 30 seconds the teacher says, "Pause . . . and look this way!"
Direction: "Thank your partner for sharing, and take your seats!"

Over the years, I have found PVF a powerful way for students to process new information just presented in a mini-lecture, or to summarize something they have been studying for a few days. One key to success here is for the teacher to move around the room listening to the various conversations. By doing this, the teacher can determine if at the end of the first two minutes there is any need to go on to the second and third stages. Students who know the teacher is constantly moving and listening are far more likely to discuss that which the teacher desires to have discussed, rather than talking about Friday night's homecoming game or dance. Listening to students who are standing, I have found, is much easier than bending over time and again to pick up on conversations between or among students who are sitting. If there is a written activity as a follow-up to PVF, the students will have been standing for long enough to make sitting down a nice change of pace.

One key to success with PVF is to make certain that the topic is broad or open enough to allow for a good deal of discussion. Also, teachers need to listen carefully for a drop in volume or body language that shows students are winding down their conversations, especially during the sixty-second segments. Sixty seconds is a long time, and teachers need to make some adjustments, if necessary, based on what they hear or see during the discussions. There is no need to drag out to a full minute a conversation that is obviously winding down.

Change Partners (and Questions)

I use this quite often, and it is an extremely flexible way of having students anticipate a new topic or summarize the information in an old one. Teachers can begin by having each student find a partner other than someone in his or her table group. Once they are paired, the teacher can ask them to discuss a question related to a topic about to be introduced, or to wrestle with some information the class has been working with for the past ten or fifteen minutes. Again, the teacher becomes a process facilitator, moving around the classroom and listening. Once that topic has been discussed by the existing pairs, the teacher can instruct the partners to thank each other and then find a new partner somewhere in the room. When the new pairs are established, they can be instructed to discuss a new topic or deal with something related to what was just discussed. Both conversations can then segue into an entirely new lesson or effectively wrap up classroom coverage of the previous one.

Replacing the Worksheet

One of my high school English teachers occasionally gave us a single-page worksheet with about twenty sentences or fragments. Our job, in a given amount of time, was to determine where the grammatical problems were in the twenty items. The whole exercise was easy for me, because I loved grammar, and I enjoyed the challenge of finding what was amiss on those sheets. For someone who did not find the going so easy, the worksheets could be frustrating. It was a quiet, individual exercise and each of us looked at the worksheet through only one set of eyes: our own. If my teacher gave us twenty minutes to complete the worksheet, some were done quickly, while others did what they could and then disengaged mentally for the remainder of the time. There was no interaction; indeed, any kind of assistance was discouraged.

Armstrong (2006) says that if what we want is kids who can use their imaginations and curiosity to explore the world around them, this won't be accomplished by "completing disposable worksheets that involve filling in the blank; circling true or false; choosing a, b, c, or d; or drawing an arrow from something in column a to something in column b" (p. 101). In active classrooms, worksheets are anathema and are used only occasionally, if at all.

If we as teachers want to check quickly for student understanding of something related to grammar, rather than use an individual pencil-and-paper worksheet, why not ask the students to stand? Then students can gather in groups of three or four where they can all see the screen for the overhead projector or an interactive white board. Display on the screen six sentences. One of the six sentences is complete and correctly written, but the other five have grammatical problems that need to be addressed. It might look something like this:

Figure 3.8   Six Sentences

Me and Samantha will attend the concert together.
Holly and Fred will go, to.
I'll pay for there tickets.
Its a good thing I'll recieve my paycheck tomorrow.
The concert should last no more than two hours
I have no doubt we'll all have a great evening.

Working in their small groups, students discuss which sentence looks right and what grammatical mistakes appear in the others. While the students are working on the problems (and solutions), the teacher circulates around the room listening to the conversations. After it appears that most groups are done (or nearly so), she can replace the image in Figure 3.8 with that in Figure 3.9, instructing them to compare what they see on the screen with what they discussed. How many errors did they find? Were there any surprises? Do they have questions?

Figure 3.9   Six Sentences With Solutions

> Me and Samantha will attend the concert together.
> Samantha and I will (shall) attend the concert together.
>
> Holly and Fred will go, to.
> Holly and Fred will go, too.
>
> I'll pay for there tickets.
> I'll pay for their tickets.
>
> Its a good thing I'll recieve my paycheck tomorrow.
> It's a good thing I'll receive my paycheck tomorrow.
>
> The concert should last no more than two hours
> The concert should last no longer than two hours.
>
> I have no doubt we'll all have a great evening.

This whole activity will probably take no more than five minutes at most, but it accomplishes at least three important things:

1. It gets students up and moving. Students who have been sitting for ten or fifteen minutes may need an opportunity to move and stretch.

2. This activity allows students to look at the six sentences *through more than one set of eyes*. Those who know exactly what was incorrect have the opportunity to teach it to someone else. Those who simply aren't sure are provided with a chance to run their suggestions by others in their group.

3. At any point during the activity (or after it is all over), the teacher, having listened in on several conversations, has the option of briefly explaining something that may be stumping many of her students as they grapple with the grammatical principles contained in the six sentences.

Finally, as the teacher listens to the conversations taking place around the room, she can determine whether or not there is a need to revisit one or more points at a later time, or to clarify what seems to be a general misunderstanding about something on the screen. This activity takes far less time than a traditional worksheet and can accomplish more in a shorter period of time.

Distribution Dipstick

Before looking at this minor formative assessment strategy, let's explore a relatively mundane, but quite normal, activity that takes place on a regular basis in most classrooms. Every teacher finds it necessary to distribute handouts, booklets, texts, and other materials during a typical week. The time-honored tradition of walking along in front of the rows of student desks, counting out the number of items that need to be distributed, takes time and can be a relative waste of time for everyone involved. I distributed materials just that way many times and considered it a necessary part of the job of teaching.

Allen (2002) suggests a number of strategies for distributing resources in a classroom, one of which involves giving each of four students a stack of workbooks (for example) and sending them to the four corners of the room. Once the four helpers are in place, the teacher would address the rest of the class:

> "Located in each corner of the room is someone who is holding your workbooks. If you would like to have one of these, your task is quite simple. Just approach one of these people and give them a compliment! If they like your compliment, they'll give you one. If not, you might have to go see someone else!" (p. 75)

I have used this distribution method frequently and have suggested that teachers use it to quickly check for understanding with students. I call this variation of the strategy the Distribution Dipstick, and it comes from a seminal event in my adolescence, an event that was (and still may be) a rite of passage for students in their mid to late teens: purchasing a car.

When I was seventeen, I worked at a supermarket in my home town in Pennsylvania. As I recall, I made a whopping ninety cents an hour working about thirty-five hours or so per week. I lived with my aunt across town and had to have her drive me to work after school and on weekends. Of course, the moment finally came when I told my aunt that if I only had my own set of wheels, she would no longer have to drive me to work, nor would I have to suffer the embarrassment of mooching a ride with friends who had cars.

Having convinced her that I needed my own transportation, she drove me to the General Motors dealership outside of town one day after work. The salesman and I were looking at the used car lot (at ninety cents an hour and working only part time, a pre-owned vehicle was my only option—and a long shot at that) when I spotted it. The car wasn't even in the lot, but out in the tall grass behind the dealership—on blocks! Eighty dollars later I drove away in a 1962, sea foam green Chevy Biscayne, a wonderful car that had only one drawback: It used oil at a prodigious rate. I had to check the oil using the *dipstick* every other day, a concession that saved me a great deal of money in the long run, since I could top off the oil when necessary and avoid bigger problems down the road.

In education we give major tests and quizzes (summative), but sometimes fail to make frequent minor (formative) checks that would, if done frequently, let us know if the students are where they should be on the road to those larger and more formal assessments. These minor and far less time consuming "dipstick" checks can inform both teacher and student as we move through chapters, units, and grading periods. All of which brings us to a simple, interesting way to conduct that dipstick check fairly frequently and quite painlessly.

This short activity, Distribution Dipstick, involves everyone in the room and gets students up and moving even as it permits the teacher to check for understanding while meandering purposefully and listening in on the various conversations. Below are the steps for the strategy.

1. The teacher needs to decide exactly what she wants to check, and it should be something fairly simple and straightforward. For example, a social studies teacher might want to know if students remember the three branches of government (executive, legislative, and judicial) and their basic functions.

2. She next gives each of *four student helpers* a sheet with the three branches of government and their functions on it and sends one helper to each corner of the room.

3. Once the helpers are in place, the teacher gives the following instructions: "When I say go, please find one of the helpers and verbally list for them the three branches of government and their individual functions. Once you have done this, you will receive from the helper a full-color chart on how bills become laws. When you receive your handout, please be seated and begin looking over the chart. Ready? Go!"

4. Once a student has provided the information, the helper thanks him or her, and provides the handout, booklet, or study guide that the teacher wants distributed. If the answer the student gives is incorrect, the volunteer can correct him and then give him the handout. (Don't let volunteers withhold the handout because of an incorrect answer.) The student

then takes the handout, proceeds to his seat, and begins to read or work on it until the activity runs its course.

So, *the handouts get distributed*; the students have a chance to stand and move about the room; the helpers have the opportunity to do a little coaching and teaching; and the teacher (in just a few short minutes) can check for understanding *by doing nothing more than monitoring the interactions taking place in the corners of the classroom*. Once more, the real work shifts from the teacher to the students while the teacher becomes a facilitator of process.

Final Thoughts on Managing Movement in the Classroom

Movement provides a change of pace for students and enhances the learning process. Students experience three distinct phases of movement during all three of the strategies introduced in this chapter: 1) standing and forming a pair or small group; 2) sharing with the partner(s); and 3) finding their way back to their seats. There is something that will help *facilitate* that movement: music—music while they travel, music while they share, and music to wrap up a discussion. It is the subject of Chapter 4.

4

Using Music to Facilitate Process

Several years ago, I spent two days in the seminar of a wonderful presenter.
His timing was impeccable, and the seminar was informative and interactive.
Time went by quickly, and it was difficult to leave at the end of the two days.
He was as aware of the overall dynamics of an audience as anyone I have ever
observed. There was only one thing missing. As we went to and returned from
breaks and as we moved into activities and paired up to process information,
songs kept playing in my head: up-tempo selections, rock, rhythm and blues,
60s pop tunes. What was missing was music. The timely and effective use of
music would have made what was a great workshop even better.

I am aware that the teachers, administrators, and staff developers who read this book often provide professional development for colleagues in the form of workshops and seminars. In a ninety-minute block, a fifty-five minute class period, a two-hour seminar, or a one-day workshop, music has many roles to play in our schools and in the professional development of educators. Therefore, in this chapter I'll speak to those who teach students and those who serve as presenters for the kind of professional development activities that support those teachers.

Music provides energy to classrooms and seminars. Music can also lighten up and energize faculty and committee meetings. Music can add just the right mood and create an atmosphere in which discussion thrives. The use of just the right song at just the right time brings smiles (and the occasional groan) to the faces of students and adult participants alike. Teachers who use music regularly in the classroom spend a great deal of time thinking about which songs might go with which activity or transition, or about what song mix will serve to put an audience in just the right mood first thing in the morning or just after lunch.

Many teachers go to school early in the morning to set themselves up mentally for the day. And a good many presenters at conferences, seminars, and workshops show up early for the same reason: to prepare for what lies ahead by "reading" the room, checking sound systems and room temperature, arranging and rearranging desks and furniture, and choosing just the right personal attitude—all in order to increase the likelihood of success. Music is the perfect accompaniment to these pre-presentation preparations. With a laptop or an iPod or any MP3 player, teachers can set up a file of music composed of the songs that are guaranteed to put us in a great mood, essential in dealing with middle school students and adult learners alike. Listening to the music we love serves to put us in a great frame of mind for a day of instruction.

If music puts the teacher or presenter in a better frame of mind, the same can be said of students and seminar participants. Approaching a room where music is playing says that something different or unusual is going on in the room. Powerful teachers and presenters greet students and participants at the door to the room and circulate among those already seated, learning names, and making connections, all to the accompaniment of appropriate music.

It is interesting to see how students (on the first day of school) or seminar participants (especially at an early-morning session) approach the classroom from the corridor or hallway. If their expectation is that theirs will be a passive role and that the main mode of delivery will be lecture, music helps begin to change that expectation as it puts learners in a better frame of mind. They begin to think that this experience is going to be somehow different. That new expectation makes it easier for the classroom teacher or seminar presenter. I once had a seminar participant admit to me at the end of our day together that she came to the seminar anticipating "the same old thing," only to end up having a great experience—at least in part due to the upbeat music used during the course of the day. A middle school teacher told me that once she began using music at the beginning of every class, the number of students late to class dropped to zero in a matter of days.

Music can be the catalyst to a great learning experience, but it takes a great deal of planning to make it work effectively. Below are a few more ways in which the use of music can enhance the classroom experience.

Music to Support and Provide Structure for Breaks

It is necessary to give learners time to "unplug" and simply switch gears for a few minutes before turning to new material or changing to a new activity. This is as true in a ninety-minute high school block as it is in a two-hour session with adult participants. Even if a time limit for the break is announced, class participants may get involved in conversations and forget about the time.

Some teachers or seminar presenters will announce that the session will resume in two minutes, and then give everyone a verbal one-minute warning. This might serve the teacher well in a classroom where no one has left the room during the break, but in an adult-learning situation it presents some problems. In an adult setting, where the participants have gone to use the restrooms or engage in a conversation in the hallway, not everyone hears the one-minute warning. The first indication that the break is over may be when those in the hallway suddenly become aware that things in the seminar room have gotten quiet. Even those in the classroom, present when the teacher announced the impending end of the break, may have been so deep in their own conversations that they did not hear what was said.

Music can come to the rescue once again in the form of what Allen (2002) refers to as a call-back song (p. 88). Many teachers or seminar leaders will introduce a song (something highly recognizable and decidedly upbeat) and inform the students or seminar participants that, when they hear that particular song, it is time to finish their conversations and return to their seats. When most of the participants are back in their seats (and while the song is still playing), one effective strategy is to pause the music and have everyone turn to his shoulder partner and say, "Welcome back!" Or, if the next step in the learning process for that session is to turn to the textbook, workbook, handout, or binder, simply say, "Please turn to page twenty-two in your binder!"

and give them some time to accomplish that. Meanwhile, the volume of that call-back song can then be turned up and then cut off. The sudden silence gets the attention of an audience far better than anything the presenter can say or do (Allen, p. 85).

I use music to work my way *into* a break as well. For example, there is a great 50s tune, *See You Later Alligator*, by Bill Haley & the Comets. After announcing the first break of the day during a one-day seminar, I establish the amount of time for the break and (with the song cued up) say, "I'll see you in ten minutes. Until then . . ." and I hit the pause button on the remote, at which point (and at a high volume) everyone hears that high-pitched voice say "See you later, Alligator!" As soon as I hit the pause button, I wave and smile. . . . The rest of the songs that play during the break end with the designated call-back song. Music takes us out, music plays during the break, and music brings us back in.

So far, then, I have suggested using music as preparatory to starting the class or as an attitude-builder. The creative use of music for breaks can provide structure and save time, getting participants back on time and ready to go for the next session or learning module. Music can also be invaluable in the learning process as students and other participants interact with each other in pairs or in groups of three or more.

Music to Enhance Discussions and Support Activities

It is no secret that some students and adult participants enjoy speaking in front of a group more than others. Anyone who has spent any time at all attempting to facilitate conversations in groups knows that there are those who simply do not feel comfortable sharing with a large number of people, especially if it amounts to a solo act. It is much easier to use a strategy like Lipton & Wellman's (2000) Paired Verbal Fluency (Chapter 3) to get students to engage in a structured discussion in pairs and then (later on) to increase the number of participants in the discussion group to three or four.

Another way to get everyone in the room involved in discussion is through the use of a tried-and-true strategy like *Think-Write-Pair-Share*. Teachers and other facilitators of group process are familiar with this interactive strategy, but let's see how it might be enhanced with the use of music.

Think-Write-Pair-Share

Most teachers don't hesitate to ask questions in the classroom. The problem comes when we try to wait any length of time for an answer. Waiting is not something teachers like to do. Indeed, we will often jump at the first hand that is raised, so anxious are we to get the "correct" answer. Every teacher and presenter has a "fan club" of those who seem to have all the answers, those who will respond at a moment's notice. If teachers are willing to work only with students who are quick to process, others who need more time to think will fold their cards early in the game. If this goes on regularly, then there are those in the class or audience who will permanently disconnect. These students and participants simply will not participate when they understand that time is rarely going to be available for them to process.

Rowe (1986) cites research that makes a case for providing adequate wait time. She concludes that "the quality of discourse can be markedly improved by increasing to 3 seconds or longer the average wait times used by teachers after a question and after a response" (p. 48). I suggest teachers stick to open-ended questions that allow plenty of latitude in terms of answers and stay away from closed questions that allow for only one or two correct answers. Teachers then need to train themselves to wait, giving everyone a chance to process.

I rarely play any music at all during this phase of the strategy. There are, I have found, many students and seminar participants for whom music is too great a distraction during this *Think* phase. I do know teachers who use Baroque music as a backdrop while their students are thinking. My best advice is for teachers to conduct this phase *with* and *without* music and see which works best.

Think-Write-Pair-Share

This next step facilitates "a shift from internal engagement to an external product which focuses the interaction, and which [the teacher] can use to monitor learning" (Lipton & Wellman, 2000, p. 86). The students now have the opportunity to capture their thoughts on paper. The teacher is active during this phase, traveling around the room, observing, and assessing understanding by reading what is being written.

Music can be added to this phase of the activity. My suggestion is that teachers stick to light jazz (Earl Klugh) or classical (Mozart) as background music, and the volume be kept low. As stated above, the teacher's job at this point is to move around the room. This makes a remote a must so that the volume can be adjusted, if necessary, as the teacher circulates. When it appears that almost everyone has written all they are going to write, the volume of the music can be brought up and cut off quickly as a signal that the next step in the process is about to begin.

Think-Write-**Pair**-Share

The thinking and writing phases are critical in giving precious minutes to those who need time to process, gather their thoughts, and then commit them to paper. How much any student or participant has written is less important than the fact that everyone has something to share with a partner in the next phase of the strategy. For this next step in the process, students and participants should work with one other person in order to share out loud what they have written.

The music now changes from classical or light jazz to something more upbeat (light 60s or 70s Pop, for example), and the volume can be increased in order to provide a musical "pad" behind the group conversations (Allen, 2002). In fact, "the use of light background music effectively 'pads' the room so that the sound from one group will not interfere with the sound from another group" (p. 86). In the absence of this "padding" (in a quiet room, for instance) one group may very well distract another.

Think-Write-Pair-**Share**

The first three phases of this activity serve as preparation for the final phase. In this last step, students and participants feel comfortable sharing with the entire group because they had a chance to *think* first, *write* down their thoughts, and then *pair* with one other person before moving on to what many human beings hate to do: speak in front of a group or audience. My experience is that the number of people willing to share *after those first three steps are successfully completed* increases significantly over the number who will share *without* this kind of preparation.

If students are going to share with the entire group and have not experienced success with this in the past, one way to overcome that is to circulate around the room during the *Write* phase. Teachers can choose three or four really good written comments and ask each of the writers in turn if they would mind sharing a particular written entry with the entire group. If they say yes, the teacher can remember their names, and during the *Share* phase, come back to them so they can share out loud with the class. Some may indicate they do not want to share, and that is fine. Make sure they understand you are perfectly okay with them not doing so. By choosing students who do not usually share with the group and knowing full well that what they have written down is a winner, they can perhaps finally taste something they may not ordinarily taste: success.

Clearly, although this strategy takes some time, it helps students build confidence; and to those who normally don't participate because they don't process quickly, it provides time to think about the question or topic, write down as many responses or comments as they think they can, test their responses out with a partner under cover of some music, and *then* possibly share with the entire class.

Give One/Get One

One effective way of getting everyone to participate and share as many responses as possible is to use a strategy called *Give One/Get One*. From the list each student or seminar participant made during the Write phase of *Think-Write-Pair-Share*, have each write his or her best idea on a sticky note. Inform them that the ideas should be written legibly, so that another member of the class can read it easily.

Once each sticky contains a single idea or response, each student should pair up with someone *other than* the partner with whom they shared in the *Pair* phase. These new partners should, when the music begins, share their ideas with each other. When they are finished, *they should exchange stickies* and each should raise his or her hand while looking for other raised hands around the room. Having found someone else who has his or her hand raised, these new partners will then share the new ideas and continue to look for other partners (and other ideas) until the teacher brings it to a halt. The purpose here is to expose students or seminar participants to as many responses or ideas as possible. The right music (upbeat) provides a perfect background for the discussion. When the teacher wants everyone to finish, it is necessary only to raise the volume of the music for a couple of seconds and then cut it off.

Finally, the stickies can be placed on the wall for review later on by everyone in the class. The stickies can (then or later) be categorized into general themes or key ideas that can serve as the basis for discussion down the road. While the stickies are being placed on the wall, a process that takes time, an upbeat song that everyone recognizes (and with which they may just sing along) can be used to accompany process. Once everyone is seated, the volume can be brought up and then be cut off to signal that the teacher needs every-one's attention, or that another activity is imminent.

The Role of Music in Choosing Learning Partners

Often, a teacher or seminar leader comes face to face with a situation where having people stand up, find a partner, and process informa-tion through discussion is desirable, even though it was not planned. A great time for this kind of random pairing is when teachers notice that students have been sitting for ten or fifteen minutes of direct instruction and need to process the information. In this case the teacher can simply instruct participants to stand up, find someone with whom they have not yet discussed anything, and introduce themselves. Upbeat tunes (*Respect*, by Aretha Franklin, for example) are perfect for getting students up and moving.

When everyone is in pairs or groups, the teacher can simply hit the pause button and say, "With your partner or partners, please dis-cuss . . .!" Once the instructions are complete, the music begins again, and the teacher circulates (with remote in hand or in pocket), giving some additional instructions when the time is almost up: "You still have fifteen seconds." The volume then increases for a very short time and the music is cut off. Partners are asked to thank each other and are instructed to move back to their seats (to the accompaniment of a new song).

Movement of participants within the room provides the perfect opportunity for the use of music that is extremely familiar to every-one. If participants are simply moving from one location to another, the lyrics can't get in the way of productive thought. I have seen peo-ple "groove" (rather than simply move) to their seats, ready to deal with whatever comes next.

Choosing Music

In *Top Tunes for Teaching: 977 Song Titles & Practical Tools for Choosing the Right Music Every Time* (2005b), Eric Jensen identifies songs to go with every occasion in the classroom. For example, Jensen's list of upbeat energizers includes *Happy Together* (The Turtles), *Shining Star* (Earth, Wind, and Fire), *At the Hop* (Danny and the Juniors), and *Do Wah Diddy Diddy* (Manfred Mann) (pp. 37, 43). These are all familiar tunes; students' parents or grandparents might listen to them, so the kids may have come into contact with them from an early age. An amazing number of songs from the 60s and 70s are showing up in commercials, movies, and television shows.

There comes a time when every teacher wants to celebrate success in the classroom: a particularly high set of test grades, an individual award for a student, the conclusion of a particularly successful field trip, a sixteenth birthday, or raising a record amount of money for charity. Tunes that might accompany a short celebration in the classroom include *I'm So Excited* (The Pointer Sisters), *Celebrate* (Three Dog Night), *We Are the Champions* (Queen), and *Celebration* (Kool and the Gang) (Jensen, 2005b, p. 41).

When I taught seventh grade, I used classical music as a backdrop for a study hall at the end of the day. I played mostly Baroque music and Mozart and Vivaldi were regular contributors to the general atmosphere in that seventh-period class. One day one of my students raised her hand and reminded me that I had forgotten to turn on the music. I asked her what she would prefer and she responded, "How about the Vivaldi?" Once I recovered from the shock of a seventh-grader asking me to play classical music, I asked her if she would prefer *Spring*, *Summer*, *Winter*, or *Fall* from Vivaldi's *Four Seasons* composition.

Teachers who play different kinds of music are often planting seeds, albeit unintentionally. My junior high school music teacher used to play classical music for us at least a couple of times per week. We seventh-graders grimaced, groaned, and otherwise resisted Beethoven, Mozart, Schubert, Rachmaninoff, and the other great classical composers. As an adult, and shortly before that former music teacher passed away, I had the opportunity to thank him for hanging in there with the classics. He planted the seeds early, and I am forever grateful.

For those interested in reading more about music in education, Rich Allen (2002) includes a sixteen-page section on the multiple uses of music in the classroom. Eric Jensen (2000b) speaks directly to "music's positive effects on the brain" (p. 1). Jensen (2005b) also provides examples of song titles that might be used for specific classroom uses and situations.

Finally, for teachers looking for songs related to a specific theme or subject, Jeff Green has compiled *The Green Book of Songs by Subject* (2002). This book lists over 35,000 songs in nearly 1,800 subject categories. A science teacher doing some planning on a photosynthesis unit might discover some useful music related to the sun (*Walking on Sunshine*) or the color green (*Bein' Green*) that can be worked into the lessons. A double indexing system makes subjects easy to find.

Technology

Many presenters and teachers find it sufficient to use CDs in the classroom, and CD players are available in almost every price range. The CD player should be a top-loader and should come with a remote. The use of the remote allows the teacher or seminar leader to be almost anywhere in the room. With the remote one can pause, adjust the volume quickly, and stop the music on command. Having a top-loading CD player makes it possible to switch CDs fairly quickly. Machines with multiple-disc capabilities simply slow down the operation when speed is essential.

More and more teachers are moving to iPods and other music players that allow the creation of whole files for specific situations. For example, a file can be set up for use when participants or students begin to arrive in the morning. As participants come back from lunch at a seminar, a separate file can be used. Other files can be created for a whole set of activities related to a specific topic, or for the morning or afternoon of an all-day session. A completely different file can be set up for use at the end of the seminar or class as participants mix with each other and exit the room.

Final Thoughts on Using Music in Classrooms

Many great teachers would benefit, as would their students, from the use of music. Those who incorporate music into their classrooms add a new and dynamic dimension to what may already be an excellent learning environment. Used effectively, music can help transform a classroom from passive to active in a short period of time.

In Chapter 5 we will move to a discussion of the role of the teacher as presenter. We'll look at the teacher's use of vocal variety, gestures, eye contact, appropriate humor, movement, wait time, body language, and more.

5

Presenting With Confidence

I once observed a seminar facilitator who used an overhead projector for a full ninety minutes, basically reading from the transparencies as they appeared on the screen. After the first break (which was much appreciated by the audience), the facilitator turned on the projector once again and then paused expectantly, waiting patiently for the participants to stop talking and seat themselves so that the seminar could resume. Nothing happened. Finally, the facilitator began to say things like, "Okay . . . if we could all be seated . . . please turn to page six in your handout. . . ." This was all said quietly and hesitantly, as if the seminar leader simply did not want to bother anyone. Slowly, at the speed of a freight train clearing a crossing, the participants began to respond and, within a minute or so, return to their seats. It was painful to watch and even more painful because I was a participant in the seminar. Many of the adult participants departed during the break, and I can't say I blamed them. They felt their time was precious and their needs as learners were not being met.

The seminar I described was for adults who *chose* to attend. The lack of that seminar facilitator's basic presentation skills caused many to leave and go elsewhere. Those who stayed (including me) did so because the information was valuable enough that we made a choice to hang in there despite the shortcomings of the presenter. Unfortunately, students don't have the luxury of being able to vote with their feet. School attendance is compulsory, and any skill deficit on the part of a teacher is just bad luck for students . . . and something to be endured. Compulsory attendance policies are not likely to change, so teachers are left with one obvious and perfectly achievable solution: improving their own presentation and facilitation skills.

During my undergraduate years, there were a number of college instructors who were adroit presenters and so served as models for those of us in the teacher preparation program who needed all the help we could get. My favorite professor was a great storyteller. Another was a great questioner who taught by dealing in universal concepts rather than strictly factual information. Others simply read from their notes in class. In one course, the professor had us each choose a partner and then assigned chapters for us to teach during the course of the semester. How we taught the chapter was up to us and most of the time we simply imparted the information in a format that too often centered on the most-modeled method of delivery to which we had access: lecture. In planning our presentations for that course, we concentrated on distilling the chapter information and regurgitating it when our turn came. Our preparation focused on content, in part because we had little knowledge about (or experience with) multiple methods of delivery.

Content is (obviously) critically important to teaching, but as Allen (2002) reminds us, we teach *people*, not content, whether we are working with students in a school or college setting, or with adults in a seminar.

> The critical issue is that if the needs of the people in the group are interfering with learning the content at a particular time, then the quality of subsequent instruction is greatly reduced. Responding immediately to the requirements of a group, or an individual, will allow for enhanced concentration on the part of participants. All learners are people first, and adapting to meet their needs respects them as unique individuals. (p. 13)

In planning for the seminar I related at the beginning of this chapter, our facilitator apparently did not take into account the physical and mental needs of the audience and used the overhead projector as a crutch for the better part of three hours.

Presenting and managing process in a confident manner requires a good deal of work and an awareness, on the part of the presenter, of specific and critical presentation skills that will help facilitate learning. The role of the teacher as presenter is something that cannot be overlooked in building the interactive classroom. This chapter will outline some basic skills that will assist teachers in making themselves better and more confident presenters. Quite often in this chapter I will use the term presenter and teacher interchangeably.

Teacher Movement

Hoff (1992) has given presenters three great reasons to move from place to place in the classroom:

1. The audience is more likely to pay attention if the presenter is not glued to one spot. Their eyes (and heads) will follow the movement of the presenter. According to Hoff, "Since physiologists tell us that 80 percent of all human motivation is optically stimulated, you'd be silly not to give [the eyes of the audience] a little workout." (p. 85)

2. Movement reduces stress on the part of the presenter. (Exercise reduces stress, and movement is exercise.)

3. Proximity is a great management tool and moving among the audience "gives everybody a feeling of participation." (p. 85)

The use of proximity is a favorite tool of teachers and in the first chapter we looked at its effectiveness as a discipline strategy. Proximity has another use related to classroom management. For example, once a student begins to answer a question, the teacher can *move away* from the student. Increasing the distance between teacher and student forces the student to speak louder (Smith, 2004) and allows the teacher to observe and monitor the rest of the class in the process. So, moving *in* causes a student to speak more softly and moving *away* has the opposite effect.

Many teachers identify locations in the room that serve specific functions when they are in presentation mode. For example, Grinder (2000) points out that given the fact that "80% of communication is nonverbal, the need to control the microphone can be done by having two locations: one for the presentation and the other for handling/ encouraging questions" (p. 176). A teacher may present some information in lecture mode from a specific position in the classroom. To make it clear to the students when they will be able to ask questions, he may then actually move a few steps away to a *second location* in the room and take those questions. After using this strategy several times, it would no longer be necessary to actually *ask* for questions. The fact that the teacher has moved to that position in the room is enough to indicate that the floor is open for students who have comments or questions.

Having a stool or captain's chair in the room (for storytelling), a fixed position front and center in the room (for bringing everyone back), and a chart and chart stand in a corner or off to the side (in yet another location in the room) allows the teacher to take advantage of the entire classroom and not stay anchored in one place. Moving to the stool alerts the audience to the fact that the teacher is about to move into storytelling mode. Moving to the "power position" in the front of the room signals that the teacher wants the attention of the students.

There comes a time when teachers introduce a topic or say something that encounters resistance from students. If the teacher is at the board and anticipates that resistance is coming, Grinder (2000) suggests that the teacher might move to another part of the room to acknowledge the resistance, and then move back to the board to continue the lecture or regular discussion once the resistance has been acknowledged and dealt with (pp. 48–49). Some teachers will have a separate location in the room for handling discipline issues. Moving there avoids "contaminating" the location from which the teacher normally lectures or leads class discussions.

Many classrooms (college and otherwise) still have lecterns as part of the furniture. Hoff (1992) reminds us that lecterns "put obstacles between you and your audience when you should be doing everything in your power to clear all obstacles away" (p. 81). Moving behind the lectern may signal the approach of a lengthy lecture, causing students to slide toward disengagement. My suggestion is to get rid of the temptation by getting rid of the lectern.

Visual Paragraphing

A useful construct for getting students or adults to remember three or four key points is something called visual paragraphing (Garmston, 1997). In working with adults and students, I have found this strategy particularly effective because it is at once visual and auditory. It involves a deliberate (and silent) move to a new position on the part of the teacher. The movement signals to the audience that a transition is imminent (Garmston, p. 92). Visual paragraphing can be used "when marking transitions within stories or content segments" (Garmston & Wellman, 1992, p. 66). It is also a great way to establish in the minds of students or adult participants the three or four outcomes for the class period or unit. In three steps, it might look like this:

1. Positioned in the front of the room and slightly to the left of center, the presenter raises her *forefinger* and announces the first purpose, expected outcome, or reason for today's lesson. "The first expected outcome today is. . . ."

2. She then takes a (silent) sideways step to her right (back to front and center in the classroom), raises *two* fingers and says, "The second expected outcome of our time together today is. . . ."

3. With one more (silent) step to the right and with *three* fingers raised, she says, "Our third and final outcome today is. . . ."

Having gone through the visual paragraph once, I will move back to that first position and say, "And number one was _____?" Moving to each position in turn and letting the audience repeat each outcome assists them in committing it to memory, at least in the short term. When using the visual in all three positions (one finger, then two, then three) it is important that the presenter look not at the audience but at her own raised finger(s). Whatever the presenter looks at is what the audience will look at. It is the visual that provides the anchor in their minds. My experience is that, having used the visual paragraph technique *at the beginning* of the day or class period, participants will need *only the visual* to identify all three outcomes *at the end*.

For many reasons, then, movement on the part of the presenter is important. Purposeful movement can be accomplished more effectively if the presenter gives some thought to room arrangement. According to Jones (2007), "The most important feature of room arrangement is *not* where the furniture goes, but, rather, where the furniture *does not go*. The objective of room arrangement is to create *walkways* in order to make mobility easy. I do not mean little, narrow walkways, I mean *boulevards*" (p. 41). The teacher's desk can make movement in the front of the room difficult for the teacher. Moving it to a back corner (or out of the room altogether!) will provide everyone in the room, teacher and students, with more space to stand, meet, and communicate. Anything the teacher can do to create more floor space will assist the kind of movement and sharing essential to success in the active classroom.

Bringing Everyone Back

As we saw in the last chapter, having the music playing when people enter helps set the tone for a workshop, seminar, or class period. A couple of minutes before starting one workshop, I was crouched in front of my iPod and going over my song list for the day when I *accidentally* hit the pause button and the music stopped. I was down on one knee facing away from the audience when that happened. Almost immediately, *the room went absolutely, utterly silent*. I turned around to see that all forty participants were looking at me expectantly. We had as yet established no procedures or norms for the day; indeed, although I had been chatting with each of them in turn, I had not even introduced myself to the group, *but when the music stopped, they followed suit*.

Of course, there are other, more traditional ways for a presenter to get the attention of a group of students or seminar participants. I have known teachers who used chimes, bells, or a series of hand claps to bring students back. The most effective way I have experienced is a combination of raising a hand and saying "Look this way please!" or "Pause . . . look this way!" What is used doesn't matter as much as making sure the participants understand what is expected. This means practicing the technique until it is ingrained in the participants' subconscious, so that pausing, getting quiet, and facing the teacher will happen routinely and on cue.

Listening and Speaking

Teachers will often turn to the audience and ask for input or questions on a specific topic under discussion. In working with students or adults, I use a technique I learned from Bob Garmston (1997) that serves to keep hands from popping up after I begin to respond to the questions. I'll choose someone to go first and then place any remaining participants in response order. For example, "Thank you. Fred, I'll take your response first, followed by Sally, and then Tony." I use my palm (palm up . . . not my forefinger) to indicate Fred. As I acknowledge Sally, I use my palm as a visual indicator; same with Tony. Having done that, I concentrate on making two things happen:

1. having set the order of responses, I turn toward Fred and give him my full attention by going very still, immediately making eye contact with him; and

2. once Fred has shared, I thank him and move quickly to Sally, repeating what Garmston calls the *Stop and Look* procedure (p. 172).

It is critical that the presenter not forget Sally and Tony, *and to address them in that order*. It is embarrassing to forget that you promised they would be next. Sometimes it is a close-run thing, and I have had to apologize on more than one occasion for calling on someone out of turn. The presenter may forget, *but the participant never does*.

If eye contact is important when listening, it is also a critical speaking skill. When I am telling a story, I try to make eye contact with almost everyone in the classroom. In speaking to students or adults, I often use someone's name when making a point: "Shelley, what I have just told everyone actually happened in just that way." In telling a five-minute story I will use several names of audience members in various locations around the room. If I see that someone's attention may be wandering, I'll use his or her name next. Hoff (1992) suggests that by giving handouts to the audience when you are speaking, the eye contact will be broken as they try to read and listen at the same time. "Eye contact is so valuable. Be wary about giving it away" (p. 120).

Vocal Variety

If listening and eye contact are critical skills, the proper use of voice is something that needs to be considered by teachers in their role as presenters. My guess is that every teacher can remember a teacher or professor who spoke in a monotone or laced his conversations with "verbalized pauses," like "um" or "you know." Speaking in a monotone quickly hypnotizes students, and verbalized pauses serve to distract them to the point where they can even begin to count the number of times the presenter says "um." In either case, retention and understanding is going to be held to a minimum, and *in either case the problems can be avoided*.

On more than one occasion in the early 1990s, I had myself videotaped presenting to student and adult audiences. The tape revealed several things of which I had been unaware. First, I used verbal pauses ("um" was my favorite) with mind-numbing regularity. Second, I had a tendency to use too many hand and arm gestures, another distraction for those in the audience. Finally, I found that my voice tended to drop off at the end of many of my sentences. Over the years I have been able to correct most of these deficiencies, *but it was the videotapes that uncovered them for me*. The problems with my presentation style had been, I am certain, quite obvious to my students and adult audiences, *but not to me*.

The Mighty Pause

In a career that includes teaching, training, and educational sales, I have come to agree with Grinder (2000) that "[t]he pause is the single most powerful non-verbal signal that can be used" (p. 62). One of its most effective uses is as a replacement for verbalized pauses like "um" or "you know." A *short pause* allows the teacher to think or refocus, does the same for the students, and is not in itself a distraction.

Great comedians are master presenters, and the best of them understand the power of the pause. Jack Benny, in radio and on television, cultivated the persona of a penny-pincher. In a comedy sequence, Benny is held at gunpoint by a robber who demands of Benny, "your money or your life!" After what seems an interminable moment of silence, the robber prompts Benny once again, "I said, your money or your life!" At which point Benny replies, "I'm thinking! I'm thinking!" The audience does not wait for the response to begin laughing. I have seen and heard this routine countless times, and what amazes me is how long Benny draws out that pause. His eventual response is almost anti-climactic. It represents the masterful use of a non-verbal.

Silence can also be used to help the class refocus. My own experience as a teacher and my observations of other teachers over the years has convinced me that we sometimes talk almost incessantly *because we are not comfortable with silence*. This is why providing wait time is difficult for teachers. It also explains why, when I began using *Think-Write-Pair-Share* as an instructional strategy, I had a problem with providing enough time for the thinking phase. The silence was deafening. For periods of extended silence to be effective, the teacher is not the only person in the room who needs to feel comfortable with it. A critical stage in the formation of a class comes when they, too, feel totally comfortable with silence (Grinder, 2000).

Getting students to participate is sometimes as simple as pausing at the end of a sentence and letting them supply the last word or phrase. The teacher has to be fairly certain, of course, that the students can successfully fill in the blank. For example, to drive a point home, a teacher may say, ". . . which just goes to show you that what goes around _____." Near the end of the sentence, the teacher cups one ear with a hand and turns it toward the students, inviting them to complete the thought. It is novel, often funny, and it does, I have found, underline whatever concept I am trying to highlight.

Humor

Virtually all the great teachers and presenters I have seen and known over the years have had a wonderful sense of humor. Most of these successful and effective educators have had as a powerful tool a self-deprecating humor that served as a good model for their students and audience participants. In classrooms where healthy laughter is abundant, the environment is positive and learning is actually facilitated (Tate, 2003). Costa (as cited in Costa and Kallick, 2000) counts among humor's positive effects "a drop in the pulse rate, secretion of endorphins, and increased oxygen in the blood" (p. 36).

Some teachers are naturally funny and don't seem to have to work at it. For those among us who want to interject humor into our role as presenters in the classroom, here are some ways to do that appropriately.

1. Jensen (2000a) suggests asking students to stand (always energizing) and "practice a big group laugh" (p. 44). This can be followed by creating small group circles where students can share their favorite jokes.

2. Teachers will often come across humorous stories or anecdotes that can be shared with students. Earlier I mentioned the use of a captain's chair or stool somewhere in the classroom as the location for telling stories. This special seat could be used for any number of humorous stories, appropriate jokes or anecdotes. In fact, students could use the stool as well, having been invited by the teacher to share a humorous story or joke from that location.

3. Tate (2003) suggests students use novel ways to provide "positive feedback for correct student responses in humorous ways, such as providing applause via a hand clapper, blowing bubbles, blowing a paper horn, or high-fiving the student" (p. 40).

4. When the teacher is willing to make fun of his own mistakes, but never of anyone else's, he signals that making fun of someone else is not appropriate behavior. There have been

occasions when *my mistakes* have formed the basis for a running gag throughout a class period or even extending over several days.

5. Done (2006) says that he constantly does things to get his students to laugh, and many of those things include using different voices, using cartoons, standing on his chair, and laughing at himself over incidents the students are bound to find funny. "I always tell my students about the time I got my tie caught in the laminator. I thought I was going to die!" (p. 35).

6. Smith (2004) suggests a great method for getting back to business after an extended period of laughter. After establishing that laughter is perfectly acceptable in the classroom, the teacher can teach the students a "post-laugh" signal that communicates that it is time to get back to work (p. 94). I can remember a teacher who would purposely build the laughter to a crescendo by raising his hands palms up until the noise was just this side of deafening, and then cut it all off by dropping his hands in much the same way as a band director making sure all the musicians stopped at the same moment.

The use of appropriate humor assists in "building a climate of connectedness and safety" (Bluestein, 2001, p. 215). Sarcasm is one example of inappropriate humor. Sarcastic "remarks directed to students that demean, ease, or deride, can, at minimum, hinder or incapacitate higher level thinking" (Jensen, 1995 as cited in Tate, 2003, p. 37). Sarcasm in a classroom where the teacher is trying to move students from a passive to an active mode is counterproductive. Teachers need to model the appropriate use of humor and indicate what *will not* be tolerated.

Addressing Presentation Skills: Ten Tips for Improvement

Any list of suggestions for improving presentation skills must begin, then, with encouraging you to have someone (for me, it was our school librarian) record an entire class period or, at the very least, a portion of the lesson where you are lecturing or otherwise presenting information. Once you have the recording, grab your notebook and a pencil and settle in to observe on the screen something you don't normally get to see: *yourself in action!*

1. During the first time through the recording, watch the recorded lesson *with the sound off*. Look for hand or arm gestures that distract or seem unnecessary. Anything that seems distracting to you will have the same effect on your audience. Take some notes so you will know what to work on later. **Keep hand and arm gestures to a minimum so your message does not get lost in the visual clutter.**

2. Keep the sound off while you observe your interactions with students. For example, when listening to a student's question, responding to the question, or asking a question of your own, what do you do with your hands? Are you facing the student asking the question? Over the years, I have developed what I call a neutral position when listening to a student or member of an adult audience. It involves standing straight, placing my hands at my sides, and maintaining a neutral facial expression. As we have seen, body language can convey all sorts of messages, and many of them are not positive. **Using a position devoid of any possible negative connotation helps with communication.**

3. Next, darken the video image and listen to the audio. Listen for vocal variety—i.e. the occasional change in pitch (high or low voice). If a monotone is what you hear, take some notes again and work a little variation into your speech patterns. According to Bowman (1998), "A singsong approach, going from high to low pitch, is probably worse than a monotone and should be avoided" (p. 72). **Observe other teachers and great speakers to see how they avoid the singsong approach or the use of a monotone voice pattern.**

4. Rewind and listen again. If you hear verbalized pauses ("um" or "you know"), try to eradicate them by forcing yourself to *pause* and *take a breath* when you might ordinarily use one of them. (During a two-hour presentation, I once asked a member of my audience to count the number of times I used "um" before the break. During the break, he gave me the number: seventeen! After the break, I made a conscious effort to pause and breathe instead of using the verbal pause and cut it to five.) **Work to replace the verbalized pauses with a pause and a conscious breath. It gives you time to think and it is not distracting to your students.**

5. Rewind and view the recording normally, with both sound and picture. Look for something different. As you lectured, asked questions, took questions from students, or otherwise interacted with the class, did you work with the entire class, or did you tend to focus *on one side of the room*? (I once had a teacher approach me after a seminar, saying "Did you know that you taught to the left side of the room for most of the hour?" I was *completely* unaware I had done that, and during the second hour of the seminar I shifted positions in the room, making a conscious effort to interact in some way with participants on both sides.) **Make an effort to connect with as many students as possible during a class period. Arrange the furniture so you can get to every part of the classroom quickly and without effort.**

6. Lipman (1999) uses the term "eye behavior" to describe the role our gaze plays in telling stories. For example, "Looking up and to one side as we pause in our speech usually suggests that we are searching our memory or thoughts in preparation for speaking" (p. 26). Lipman suggests that storytellers concentrate on their relationship with the audience and on what they want to communicate, rather than on worrying too much about making eye contact X number of times (p. 27). **Make eye contact naturally as you deem appropriate.**

7. Having been through the recording a few times, did you make any observations about your own use of wait time? If you asked questions, did you allow time for students to formulate answers? After introducing a key concept or point during the class period, did you allow time for them to consider its meaning or implications? Rowe (1969, 1974, as cited in Costa & Kallick, 2000) observed positive changes in classrooms where teachers consistently used purposeful silence. This has important implications for the active classroom. The frequent and effective use of wait time leads to an increase in student confidence, speculative responses, and student-to-student interactions. It also results in a reduction in the amount of "teacher-centered show-and-tell" (p. 7). **Allow for the more frequent use of silence and purposeful wait time during classroom discussions. Your object here is to reduce the amount of talking you do even as you increase the amount of thinking and talking that your students do, shifting them from a passive to an active role.**

8. If you used an electronic slide presentation or the overhead projector, were they on during your entire presentation? There may be times when you want to depart from what is on the screen and have students interact with each other using the information you have been presenting. While they are processing and you are moving about the room, turn the overhead projector off during the discussion. Use a remote with an electronic computer presentation to darken the image on the screen. The images in both cases serve as a distraction, especially if you or a student walks in front of the screen. **Make an effort to use the images only when they are necessary and turn them off when moving to seatwork or any kind of paired or group interaction.**

9. As you viewed the tape, what did you notice about your interactions with students? Were you patient with their questions or with their answers to your questions? Did you glance at your watch while a student was speaking? Did you lose your temper at any point during the lesson? What did you note in your body language (negative, positive, or neutral)? Volume of your voice (too soft or too loud)? Furniture (or cords) that got in your way or inhibited your movement or that of your students? **You might even share with them what you observed concerning your interactions while viewing the tape. Ask them to give their impressions of your body language, vocal variety, wait time, verbal pausing, eye contact, and anything else that might be of use as you seek to improve your presentation skills. Teachers need feedback, too.**

10. With great teachers, continuous improvement is a way of life. Beginning with your notes on what you observed as you viewed yourself in action, along with the input of your students, **begin to make some changes that will improve your delivery and increase the likelihood that students will benefit from those improvements.**

Final Thoughts on Presenting With Confidence

The teacher who takes seriously the importance of improving his or her own presentation skills will subsequently model those improvements for students. In the active classroom, students are shifted purposefully from a passive to an active role. Doing that requires that they, too, improve their own abilities as they interact with the teacher and with each other in paired or group discussions. Because students may be uncomfortable in the role of presenter and communicator, we need to work with them as they develop and perfect their own communication skills.

In Chapter 6 we'll take a look at the importance of learning styles, or modality preferences, in teaching. Not everyone learns or processes information in the same way, and knowing whether students are high or low auditory, high or low kinesthetic, or high or low visual can be helpful when it comes to planning instruction. Teachers' preferences can impact instruction as well, as we'll discover.

6

Teaching to All Modalities

The year was 1993, and I was teaching on the Apple Team at Plaza Middle School in Virginia Beach. The subject was United States history, and my four classes were studying the period just prior to the Civil War. Some students were giving abolitionist speeches for their classmates. I was sitting off to the side as a young African American student made one such impassioned speech. When she was done, there was complete silence for a few seconds. Utter silence. Helen Cox, the special education teacher on our inclusion team, looked at me and our jaws raced each other to the floor. The silence was broken by what can only be described as spontaneous and sustained applause such as I have rarely heard anywhere. That thirteen-year-old special-education student had delivered a speech that reached everyone in the room. In the two or three minutes it took her to give the speech, I was once again, as is so often the case, reminded of why I had become a teacher. The tone, the pitch, the gestures, the passion . . . it was all there, and it captivated her peers and her teachers. I had been teaching the period leading to the Civil War for almost a month, and in three minutes she managed to do what I had been unable to do in three weeks. She transported us back to the 1850s and made believers of everyone in the room.

That moment is etched in my mind because of the emotion generated by her speech. That assignment surfaced in her a predilection for communication. Not everyone in the class shared that auditory strength, and few students, as I recall, chose to give a speech. Other students selected Civil War era projects more suited to their own individual talents and areas of interest. When I first started teaching in the 70s, I would not have provided the assignment flexibility I did in 1993. By giving students a choice of projects and assignments, we allow their unique strengths and natural abilities to come into play.

Not all of us, students and adults alike, learn the same way. Our learning styles, or modalities, differ. "The theory centers on the premise that individuals begin to concentrate, process, and remember new and difficult information in very different ways" (Searson & Dunn, 2001, p. 22). The implications, of course, are that teachers need to take these differences into account when planning lessons.

As teachers plan instruction, there are, according to Gregory (2005), five considerations that will make sure the needs of all learners are met:

1. creating a classroom environment to match students' preferences;

2. including instruction that appeals to all the senses;

3. facilitating social interactions;

4. differentiating levels of challenge and engagement; and

5. presenting material to appeal to auditory, visual, and kinesthetic modalities. (p. 23)

Sousa (2001) affirms that teachers strong in one modality "tend to teach the way they learn" (p. 57). In my first few years of teaching, my own predilection for the auditory led me to lecture far more than was wise. This left my students whose main learning styles were visual or kinesthetic in the dust. Actually, since I did most of the talking, even the auditory learners were not satisfied because their own need to talk was not being met.

The second and third chapters of this book underscore the value of structured conversation and movement in classrooms and provide some specific strategies for incorporating those two elements into the delivery of instruction. The fourth chapter adds music to the mix. The powerful combination of structured conversation, purposeful movement, and music can go a long way toward meeting the needs of diverse learners. Those students whose preferences are for the auditory and kinesthetic modalities are quite likely to enjoy and benefit from the strategies contained in those three chapters.

There are, in fact, many specific strategies and methods of delivery that will help meet the needs of those who process information in different ways. This chapter will serve to expand the repertoire of ways in which teachers can capitalize on the learning preferences of students. We'll look at all three traditional modalities (visual, auditory, and kinesthetic) in turn and list some ways to ensure that students can experience success in the style of learning that fits them best.

Visual Modality

Every teacher gives verbal instructions as to what is to be done or how something is to be done. Students who are highly visual will naturally appreciate directions or instructions that are written as well as verbal. Posting directions in the same place each time they are given assists visual learners and allows teachers to point to the board, screen, or chart when there are questions about procedures. Why talk and distract everyone when simply looking at the visual posting of the directions does the job? If the eyes of the student quite naturally follow the eyes of the teacher, then "once the teacher has the student's attention, the student will look where the teacher directs his eyes. If the teacher looks at the board, the student will follow his lead and look at the board also" (Grinder, 2000, p. 138).

Attending to the needs of visual learners brings up a problem with the use of overhead transparencies, PowerPoint presentations, and other visual displays. Often, teachers will display a list, picture, or other visual image. Before students have had a chance to familiarize themselves with the material being displayed, the teacher begins to talk. No matter the learning style, students will have difficulty trying to assimilate the new visual information while simultaneously listening to the teacher. Allen (2002) presents a simple solution to the problem. His advice is to pause when the image or information is revealed and "continue speaking only when it appears that everyone has seen and feels comfortable with the new information. After they have had time to construct a mental picture, they will be able to concentrate more fully on what is being said" (Allen, p. 96).

Visual learners will also appreciate graphic organizers such as the Venn Diagram (Figure 6.1). The Venn gives visual learners a solid and permanent image showing how two things, ideas, or concepts are compared and contrasted. Taking a close look at a completed Venn

Diagram, or working with another student to complete it from scratch, gives the visual learner confidence for the inevitable class discussion on the selected topic.

Figure 6.1   Venn Diagram

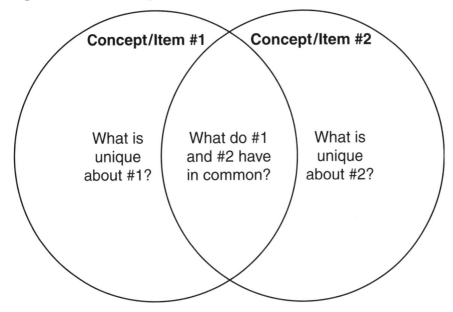

Gregory (2005) has compiled a list of ways in which the preferences of visual learners are manifested. An abbreviated listing shows that, among other tendencies or characteristics, visual learners:

- create pictures in their mind and use images to remember;
- prefer reading, writing, making notes, and diagrams;
- accurately read body language and pick up on facial expressions;
- like to use drama and art;
- make lists and write things down;
- attention may wander during verbal activities;
- exhibit upward eye movements, rapid speaking, and shallow breathing; and
- use visual language when communicating, such as "It looks right to me" or "Don't you see?" (p. 25)

Auditory Modality

Those whose "preferred sense" is hearing are auditory learners (Sousa, 2001, p. 57). The middle school student who gave the powerful abolitionist speech in my classroom in 1993 was high auditory. This does not simply mean that she enjoyed hearing others speak; she enjoyed speaking herself and experienced a great deal of success on that and other occasions where she was called upon to share verbally in class. When collaborating with other teachers or other colleagues over the years, I have often found it helpful to verbalize my thoughts and get feedback from the other members of the group. "Information isn't real [for auditory learners] until they have had a chance to discuss it" (Sprenger, 2002, p. 76).

Once again, we reach to Gregory (2005) for a partial listing of those manifestations that identify the auditory learner. Such learners

- like to be read to;
- like to learn from lectures and audiotapes;
- hum, self-talk, or subvocalize when reading;
- "sound out" when they spell;
- practice aloud and learn by talking to themselves;
- like the telephone, radio, and chatting;
- exhibit sideways eye movements, even speech, and mid-chest breathing; and
- use auditory language, such as "It sounds right" or "Listen to this." (pp. 25–26)

Kinesthetic Modality

Kinesthetic learners have a great deal of trouble in traditional (mostly auditory) classrooms. Yet the movement and physical activity they crave is directly tied to learning. Hannaford (2005) asserts that "[a]lmost daily, new research is illuminating the strong neural links between areas in the brain involved with movement and those involved with cognitive activity" (p. 110). The movement that pleases and supports kinesthetic learners tends to help all students because of the connection between movement and the growth and development of the human brain:

> A strong cerebellum is essential for efficient problem-solving skills and mental planning. Without regular physical activity,

the teen brain gets the signal that the neurons in the cerebellum aren't as important as the neurons in other places.... And without a strong and healthy cerebellum, that multi-step math problem and reflective essay are much harder to do. (Feinstein, 2004, p. 34)

Unfortunately, students tend to move and exercise less in school as they move on through the grades. Classrooms that were once set up with built-in movement, physical exercise, and hands-on activities in elementary school become secondary classrooms where, in too many cases, the desks are in straight rows and "seat work" is the norm. "Buckling down" replaces standing up in many middle and high school classrooms.

Dunn and Dunn (2005) underline the importance of using kinesthetic strategies in special education classrooms. In "experimental studies, [special-needs students] achieved statistically higher test scores when the activities required them to be physically interactive...." (p. 275).

Kinesthetic learners, then, may exhibit the tendency to:

- often use movement and are action oriented;
- seem to gesture and fidget when speaking;
- tap or drum on desk;
- seem to be impulsive;
- don't choose to read if possible;
- like to act out concepts and "do" things;
- have to write words as they spell (find spelling challenging);
- prefer sports and dancing;
- solve problems while moving;
- touch while they communicate;
- exhibit downward eye movements, deep breathing, and slow speech; and
- use language of action and feelings, such as "I feel that it's right" or "Now I get it." (Gregory, 2005, p. 26)

Suggestions Related to Multi-Modality Teaching

If teachers have an idea, then, of the characteristics or tendencies of those students who are visual, auditory, or kinesthetic, the implicit next step might be to look at what can be done to create the environment where the needs of all students can be met.

1. In Chapter 3 we looked at the importance of **room arrangement** in facilitating movement in the active classroom. There were two suggestions for arranging the furniture in order to create open space for teacher and student movement. These more-open arrangements permit the kind of movement and sharing that benefits kinesthetic learners and their teachers (who need to move quickly and efficiently from place to place in the classroom). Traditional classroom arrangement in most middle and high schools inhibits both teacher and student movement.

2. **Lesson plans** should incorporate opportunities for hands-on activities, mini-lectures, periods of structured (and simultaneous) processing, choice of projects, use of visuals, graphic organizers, and a multitude of other strategies that will tap into the learning styles of all students.

3. Teachers should become aware of the **learning styles** of students and have a discussion with them about the fact that they all process information in different ways. Students who understand that teachers will make an effort to meet those various needs are more likely to be understanding when some of the strategies used in class do not match their particular mode of learning.

4. When possible, teachers should **give students a choice** of whether they want to work alone on a class assignment or in pairs (Tomlinson & McTighe, 2006). Those who are high auditory may prefer working with a partner, but students who are low auditory may feel more comfortable working and reflecting alone.

5. Finally, teachers would benefit from knowing whether their *own* modality tends to the visual, auditory, or what Sousa (2001) identifies as tactile/kinesthetic. The checklist that follows is short and should help teachers determine what Sousa calls sensory preferences and what I have been calling learning styles or modalities.

Figure 6.2 Determining Your Sensory Preferences

This checklist indicates your sensory preference(s). It is designed for adults and is one of many that are available. You should not rely on just one checklist for self-assessment. Remember that sensory preferences are usually evident only during prolonged and complex learning tasks.

Directions: For each item, circle "**A**" if you **agree** that the statement describes you most of the time. Circle "**D**" if you **disagree** that the statement describes you most of the time. Move quickly through the questions. Your first response is usually the more accurate one.

1. I prefer reading a story rather than listening to someone tell it.	A	D
2. I would rather watch television than listen to the radio.	A	D
3. I remember faces better than names.	A	D
4. I like classrooms with lots of posters and pictures around the room.	A	D
5. The appearance of my handwriting is important to me.	A	D
6. I think more often in pictures.	A	D
7. I am distracted by visual disorder or movement.	A	D
8. I have difficulty remembering directions that were told to me.	A	D
9. I would rather watch athletic events than participate in them.	A	D
10. I tend to organize my thoughts by writing them down.	A	D
11. My facial expression is a good indicator of my emotions.	A	D
12. I tend to remember names better than faces.	A	D
13. I would enjoy taking part in dramatic events like plays	A	D
14. I tend to subvocalize and think in sounds.	A	D
15. I am easily distracted by sounds.	A	D
16. I easily forget what I read unless I talk about it.	A	D
17. I would rather listen to the radio than watch television.	A	D
18. My handwriting is not very good.	A	D
19. When faced with a problem, I tend to talk it through.	A	D
20. I express my emotions verbally.	A	D
21. I would rather be in a group discussion than read about a topic.	A	D
22. I prefer talking on the phone rather than writing a letter to someone.	A	D
23. I would rather participate in a group discussion than read about a topic.	A	D
24. I prefer going to museums where I can touch the exhibits.	A	D
25. My handwriting deteriorates when the space becomes smaller.	A	D
26. My mental pictures are usually accompanied by movement.	A	D
27. I like being outdoors and doing things like biking, camping, swimming, hiking, etc.	A	D
28. I remember best what was done rather than what was seen or talked about.	A	D

(Continued)

Figure 6.2 *(Continued)*

29. When faced with a problem, I often select the solution involving the greatest activity.   A   D

30. I like to make models or other hand-crafted items.   A   D

31. I would rather do experiments than read about them.   A   D

32. My body language is a good indicator of my emotions.   A   D

33. I have difficulty remembering verbal directions if I have not done the activity before.   A   D

Interpreting Your Score

Total number of "A" responses in items 1–11: _____
This is your visual score.

Total number of "A" responses in items 12–22: _____
This is your auditory score.

Total number of "A" responses in items 23–33: _____
This is your tactile/kinesthetic score.

If you scored a lot higher in any one area: This sense is *very probably* your preference during a protracted and complex learning situation.

If you scored a lot lower in any one area: This sense is *not likely* to be your preference in a learning situation.

If you have similar scores in all three areas: You can learn things almost any way they are presented.

Reflections

A. What was your preferred sense? Were you surprised?

B. How does this preference show up in your daily life?

C. How does this preference show up in your teaching?

Final Thoughts on Teaching to All Modalities

Teachers would do well, then, to determine what their own modality preference is, perhaps using Sousa's checklist, and ponder how it may affect their style of teaching. It makes sense that teachers should try to gauge the preferences of students in their classes as well. Employing strategies that meet the learning styles of all students will go a long way toward ensuring that those needs are met.

In Chapter 7 our topic will be the use, misuse, or overuse of visuals and technology. Advances in technology have provided wonderful teaching aids, but teachers should be careful not to let the technology replace good pedagogy in the classroom.

7

Using Visuals and Technology

In Philadelphia a number of years ago, I had the opportunity to attend the seminar of a master presenter who used visuals to great effect. In an age when electronic presentations and colorful graphics predominate, this presenter used a simple black magic marker and white chart paper to perfection. Each of the charts he created served as visual anchors for session participants, and the presenter returned to them again and again in order to reinforce concepts and information from earlier in the seminar. Unlike some PowerPoint presentations where the images come and go, perhaps with little lasting effect, these simple, strong visuals allowed presenter and audience alike to visit them time and again during the seminar.

All of the most powerful and effective teachers and presenters I know understand the impact of visuals. When the visuals are created and then posted, students and seminar participants can use them to trigger thoughts and stimulate the thinking process. Dickinson (1995) points out that visual imagery connects with students "even when no reference is made to them in discussion" (p. 263). When the presenter or teacher does make reference to visuals and allows time for seminar participants or students to contemplate and understand them, the images have even more impact.

The key to using technology may be to understand that it supports the lesson, but should not, as is often the case with PowerPoint presentations, *become* the lesson. Perhaps the most overused piece of technology available today, "the PowerPoint presentation is a small part of the whole instructional package" (F de Wet, 2006, p. 6). The *whole* instructional package may include the use of charts, graphs, overhead transparencies, artwork, student drawings and posters, blackboards, projected computer images, commercial posters, chalk, markers, maps, and videos. Interactive whiteboards are incredibly flexible and useful, and that technology is expanding at an amazing rate.

Visuals and technology, properly used, provide impact. Visuals provide clarification as well. Something described verbally in a classroom of thirty students may result in thirty different interpretations in the minds of those students. Adding the visual to the verbal clarifies thoughts and brings everything into focus. Leonardo da Vinci's notebooks are filled with about 1,500 drawings that illuminate and add visual clarity to his verbal descriptions of everything from flying machines to anatomical renderings of animals and humans (White, 2000). This has provided later generations, and not a few biographers, with a treasure trove of permanent visual images. Classroom teachers who complement the auditory with the visual can provide that same kind of impact, focus, and clarity.

In planning for the active classroom, working visuals into lessons requires that balance be achieved. The use of any one visual aid so that it dominates the lesson may reduce its effectiveness as a support mechanism. Turning out the lights, pulling down the shades, and showing anything on the screen at length will lead to predictable results with students or seminar participants of *any* age. The key is to combine all the elements (visual, auditory, kinesthetic) in such a way that students are awake, alert, and engaged. This puts us in mind, once again, of the role of teacher as orchestra conductor, successfully balancing the contributions of everyone in the orchestra to the lasting benefit of the audience.

Let's take a look, then, at some visual and technological support systems that can assist teachers with the active classroom.

Simple and Effective Visuals

Photos, graphs, charts, and maps not only add visual impact to a presentation that might otherwise be totally auditory, but are necessary additions, as we have seen, for those whose dominant learning style is visual. Incorporating visuals into instruction has other benefits as well. Something as simple as posting visual directions that can be easily seen as students enter the room can be powerful. Whatever the medium for this (blackboard or whiteboard, chart, overhead transparency), it probably helps to display it in the same manner and in the same location each day so students will know where to look.

In the 1950s, when I was growing up in Pennsylvania, black and white was the rule in photos and on television. Color was the exception. Today this is exactly reversed. Color is the norm and black and white images are rare, *and that fact can be used to a teacher's advantage*. Advertisers today will often use black and white imagery, or a single (spot) color in both print and TV advertising precisely because it is novel and catches the viewer's attention. Anything that is a novelty is particularly useful in the active classroom for that very reason. In fact, novelty "creates a stronger opportunity for new learning and pathways in the brain" (Jensen, 2005a, p. 120).

As demonstrated earlier in this chapter, a piece of white chart paper and a black marker can be particularly effective as a visual communication tool in the classroom, again because of the *stark contrast* between that simple medium and the steady diet of swiftly transitioning color images to which we have become accustomed. Garmston and Wellman (1992) suggest using charts "when you have big ideas that you want to keep present in the room for reference. These also become anchors for future sessions with this audience" (p. 69). If students are brainstorming and recording the results in lists on chart paper, using alternating marker colors is more effective when trying to subsequently view them from across the room (p. 68). Teachers can leave those simple visuals posted for days as they work with students on a given concept or unit.

Wall Posters

Commercial wall posters adorn many classrooms around the country, and most of them are indeed colorful and quite attractive. The question may be whether they have a powerful and lasting impact. My sense of this is (and I put many a poster on many a classroom wall) that commercial posters will have far more impact when students use the information on them in some way. For example, if there are several posters adorning the walls dealing with a particular topic, teachers can put kids in groups of three or four and have them visit each poster in turn while some music is playing. Each group can be directed to answer two important questions as they visit each poster in turn: 1) What does the poster mean? and 2) What does it mean to them or to the subject they are currently studying? At the beginning of the school year, a teacher could post the classroom rules separately around the room and have small groups of students visit and discuss each one in turn, following that with a general discussion of the importance of rules in the smooth running of the classroom.

I visited an elementary classroom recently where the teacher, Dana Jackson, was working with students on writing skills. The class was divided into five groups of four students each, and one of the four students in each group went into the hallway for as long as it took for Jackson to use some direct instruction on declarative sentences with the rest of the class. She gave this mini-lesson while the kids stood in front of her in the center of the room, taking notes in special "journalism" notebooks used only for that purpose. Then the kids went back to their tables to prepare to "teach" their classmates (the "students") who were about to come into the room from the hall and rejoin their groups.

That whole process of direct instruction, followed by "teachers" instructing "students" continued until the class had covered the four sentence types: declarative, question, exclamatory, and command. At that point Jackson divided them into four new groups, and they constructed their own posters that would serve as anchors for future writing assignments and classroom discussion. "Mr. Declarative Man" decorated the center of the poster dealing with declarative sentences and, one after another, the completed posters were put on the wall of the classroom. Jackson had chosen not to purchase a commercial poster because she knew her students' own work would have more lasting impact than a laminated, commercially-produced poster containing the same information. Her students' investment in the posters made them more valuable and meaningful than something professionally produced.

Deming (2000) warns that posters and exhortations that are intended to increase production in an organization may have the opposite effect. For example, a poster that says "Getting better together" in an organization where no one pays any attention to workers' suggestions for improvement simply infuriates the workers (Deming, p. 66). A poster that says "We can do this together!" in a classroom run in a highly autocratic fashion may not escape the irony meter of students in that class. In this case, of course, an otherwise beautiful poster may serve as a demotivator.

Class Run Charts

Jenkins (2003) demonstrates how one very big *visual motivator* (posted on the classroom wall) can be a class run chart showing the progress of the *entire class* over time. For example, if students have a weekly ten-point vocabulary quiz and the total number of students in the class is twenty-five, then there are 250 *possible correct answers* for every quiz. Each week's total number of correct answers is posted on a run chart and students can easily see progress over time. To keep students from cramming on Thursday night for a Friday quiz (and then quickly forgetting the material), Jenkins suggests that the *total number* of vocabulary words be written on individual slips of paper and placed in a bag. The slips of paper can be drawn randomly for each weekly quiz. This random selection takes away any suggestion of trickery on the part of the teacher "if a disproportionate number of difficult words appear on a particular quiz" (Jenkins, p. 38).

Over the course of several weeks, the class run chart for vocabulary might look like the one in Figure 7.1. Steady progress, even with some slight dips, can serve as a powerful visual motivator. Teachers can introduce the concept of the *baseline* (the first week's results and starting point) and in subsequent weeks have students discuss and ponder why the total number of correct answers dipped a bit in Week 4 (students absent? more difficult vocabulary words?) or jumped considerably in Week 9.

Figure 7.1 Vocabulary Quiz Run Chart

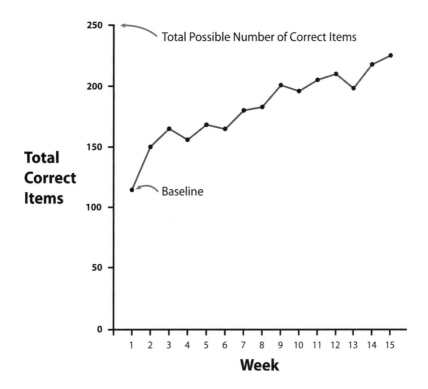

Source: Brian T. Jones.

One word of caution: Teachers who have several classes covering the same material might want to be careful not to post the run charts where the other classes can see them. One excellent middle school social studies teacher with whom I worked on this concept, Fred Alarcon, posted the run chart for each of the four classes in his eighth-grade classroom. According to Alarcon, students in the classroom with the lowest scores began to talk of themselves as the "dumb class" (personal communication, September 16, 2007). Regardless of the fact that their class had the fewest number of students, something that Alarcon explained regularly affected the results; the *visual image of the lower point total had a negative effect*. Alarcon then simply combined all four classes into one giant run chart. All four of his middle school classes were now part of the overall continuous improvement effort, and any negative competitive effects were erased. In addition, he had each student keep his or her own run chart showing individual progress throughout the year. Run charts can serve as powerful visual reminders of continuous improvement on the part of the student and the class as a whole. Not coincidentally, the scores on the year-end state assessment increased dramatically for Alarcon's students as compared with the previous year's results.

Elementary teacher Chuck Kenison regularly gathers his students around the overhead projector so that he can "unveil" the latest reading level results or math score results for the class as a whole (personal communication, September 5, 2007). The class sets regular goals, and if they don't reach the goals they discuss possible reasons why. On one memorable occasion, Kenison gathered everyone around the overhead and, without saying anything, simply displayed the new bar graph entry for January. The kids all gazed at the screen for a second and then a mighty cheer broke out from the class. They were high-fiving and hugging each other, and Kenison said he just stood there with a big grin on his face. No words he could have used would have replaced the visual that told his students they *had just surpassed their goal* for January. That simple bar graph told them they had sailed over the bar as a class. To me, that represents intrinsic motivation at its most effective—and it was totally visual.

Alarcon's middle school social studies students and Kenison's elementary students were excited because, as a group, they had continually improved (with a few bumps in the road) on the way to goals *they had set themselves*. The run charts (individual or group) served as visual indicators and powerful reminders of success. According to Jenkins (2005), this kind of observable evidence "is far more powerful than any amount of stickers, money, popcorn, or attaboys" (p. 94). Using these visuals as a focus for regular celebrations will motivate kids to stay engaged, continue learning, and keep succeeding.

Another very simple, but effective, form of visual feedback is used regularly by Joe Gentry, a high school biology teacher. When students in his classes are doing seatwork, Gentry travels around the room with a green pen (personal correspondence, September 27, 2007). Pausing long enough to see what each student is writing, he underlines anything his students have written that is correct. What he underlines may pertain to spelling, grammar, or content. According to Gentry, this simple feedback tool has at least five important advantages, in that:

1. it takes the teacher out from behind his desk and allows him to make certain everyone is on task;

2. the feedback is immediate, and the student knows before he leaves the class what he does not have to work on at some other time prior to turning in the assignment;

3. because the feedback is visual, it does not bother anyone else in the room who might be distracted by constant auditory feedback on the part of the teacher;

4. if a student has a question, asking it with the teacher right next to his desk is much more private than asking it in front of the rest of the class; and

5. if the teacher is going to grade the assignment or provide additional written feedback, a good deal of the work is already done. He can simply ignore whatever he has under-lined in green, saving time later on (personal correspondence, September 27, 2007).

Having done this for three years, Gentry has seen an improve-ment in the quality of his students' assignments related to grammar and content. He has also saved an enormous amount of his own time using a simple feedback technique that his students appreciate and on which they have come to rely.

Overhead Projectors

When I first started teaching in the early 1970s, the overhead projector was front and center in most classrooms, and I must admit to overus-ing that particular piece of equipment. I lectured a good deal, and I revealed important points one at a time on each transparency while students took notes. I shudder when I think how attached I became to that projector. I stood beside it and, as I recall, rarely moved as I expounded on one thing after another. To my great regret, I was not effective, which is not to say that overhead projectors do not have their uses. I have seen presenters and teachers use them very effectively.

In buildings where overhead projectors are supplied as a matter of course, teachers are normally assigned overhead projectors, and new teachers may simply inherit the one used by the previous occu-pant of that particular classroom. Teachers who intend to use the overhead as a visual tool need to take a close look at the projector sit-ting in the classroom when they arrive. Scratches on the glass, dust, discoloration, and any noise created by the motor can and will dis-tract students. Before using the projector, teachers should perform (or have performed for them) some basic maintenance. Clean the projec-tor inside and out, changing the glass if it contains discoloration or scratches of any kind. Put an image on the screen with the projector, and stand in the back of the room and off to the side. If the image is clear and in focus to you, it will be clear and in focus to your students. Teachers who want to use overhead projectors should never be satisfied with one that does not do the job.

Jensen (1998) has some suggestions for using overhead projectors. I have included a few of them below.

1. Check lighting in the room in advance of your presentation. Make sure that the room is light enough for participants to write while you're using the overhead, but also dark enough to see the transparencies clearly.

2. Turn off the projector when there is a break of more than fifteen seconds between overheads.

3. Use special laser pointer-markers. Avoid using your finger or hand to point. (p. 35)

Jensen also suggests protecting frequently-used transparencies by placing them in plastic holder sheets that can be stored in a binder for easy access. I have observed teachers who consistently misplace transparencies during class and, in general, display a lack of organization not lost on the students. Looking all over the front of the room for a transparency that was "there a minute ago" is disruptive at best and may result in losing the students altogether.

Teachers who have just covered some new information on the overhead should give students a chance to ask questions and then process the material (Allen, 2008, p. 95). In fact, if they have been sitting for a few minutes, have them stand up, pair up, and discuss the material. If it helps to have the images on the screen, then leave the projector on. If not, turn it off while they share. If the lights were dimmed, bring them back up for the discussion. This opportunity for student processing is what may be missing from many classroom lessons that utilize overhead projectors, PowerPoint slide shows, or any other electronic visual image.

Videos/Film

I can remember as a substitute teacher going into a high school classroom and seeing the following directions on a lesson plan: Show film/Have discussion. Showing the film was easy. Having the discussion was not, and for one very good reason: In most cases, students simply ignored the film and went somewhere else in their minds, making meaningful post-video discussion difficult, if not impossible. Unless it is one powerful video, student engagement is unlikely.

The use of films and videos in classrooms can have impact if shown in small segments that are tied to whatever is under discussion in the classroom. Sections of a documentary, for example, may supplement and support a classroom exploration of the topic; in such a case, *short clips* combined with the previous night's reading assignment might make for a great discussion with students in pairs or groups. Students who are subsequently interested in seeing the entire documentary may be able to do so on their own.

PowerPoint Usage

Everyone reading this book can probably tell a "Death by PowerPoint" story. As with the earlier technology of the overhead projector, the danger with slide presentations is that teachers allow them to overwhelm the lesson and, in the process, underwhelm the audience. Electronic presentations can be effective if they are used appropriately. My own experience as a teacher and trainer has suggested some possible tenets of effective electronic slide usage.

1. Avoid the use of "cutsie" images (dancing bears, shooting stars, etc.) that add little to your lesson and serve as powerful (and often annoying) distractions. Internet advertisers want us to see what they have to offer and will create images that blink, move, and otherwise pull our eyes to them—on purpose and perhaps to great effect for advertising. Students will be easily distracted by these "gimmicks," and their use will detract from your message.

2. Use large type and a font that is not going to get in the way of the message. I have found that Times Roman and Arial work just fine. Script fonts are often difficult to read. Type sizes should be, in my estimation, twenty point or larger. Years ago I attended a session where the presenter consistently used twelve to fourteen point type, and it was simply unreadable from my position in the back of the room.

3. When using electronic slide shows, keep the design simple. Bowman (1998) suggests that when using type, five lines of type and five words per line on each slide is best (p. 80).

4. Presenters and teachers will often have type or graphic elements "fly" or corkscrew into place on the screen. My suggestion is that a simple fade-in will do, or let it simply appear on the screen without fanfare. Remember, it is your message that is important, not how it gets to its appointed position in the slide.

5. As soon as the information is in place on the slide, pause, stand off to the side, and *let your eyes go to the image*. Your students' eyes generally will go where your eyes go.

6. Once you and your students are looking at a still image displayed on the board, chart, or screen, pause so everyone can adjust to what is being displayed. Dissonance is created when students have begun to read or otherwise concentrate and the teacher begins talking.

7. If you are using an electronic presentation, use a remote that allows you to go forward, backward, and to darken the screen altogether, temporarily removing the image so that students will return their attention to you. Otherwise, the visual image serves as competition in any discussion. An exception, of course, would be when the graphic, chart, or other image is critical to the discussion in such a way that making it disappear would short-circuit the discussion.

8. It may become necessary to dim the lights a bit in order to make certain everyone in the room can see the image clearly. If the alternative to a brightly lit classroom is a completely dark one, keep the lights on. I can remember a teacher who turned out the lights only to have the entire class (and himself) fall asleep.

9. Regardless of what kind of visuals or technology you are using, it is critical to *get it all set up before class*. Take the time to go to every part of the room and sit in the students' chairs to ensure that they will have an unobstructed view of the image(s) when they arrive. Something may have to be moved to make this possible. This should all be done before the students come into the room so that valuable *class time* is not taken up trying to rearrange the projector, the screen, the flipchart, the blinds, or the furniture.

Graphic Organizers

Parry and Gregory (1998) identify graphic organizers as "metacognitive tools in a visual form" that "allow students to organize data into manageable and comprehensible chunks" (p. 168). Teachers should not, according to Wicks, Peregoy, and Wheeler (2001), see powerful tools such as fishbone diagrams and flowcharts as add-ons, but as tools that "will help [them] tackle the curriculum—more efficiently and more effectively" (p. 167). Fishbone diagrams (Figure 7.2) help students with cause and effect and can be used in almost any subject area. Flowcharts (Figure 7.3) assist students in visualizing sequence. Students who are high visual are particularly well-served by graphic organizers, but my experience has been that students in general appreciate the efficacy of these visual tools.

Figure 7.2   Fishbone Diagram

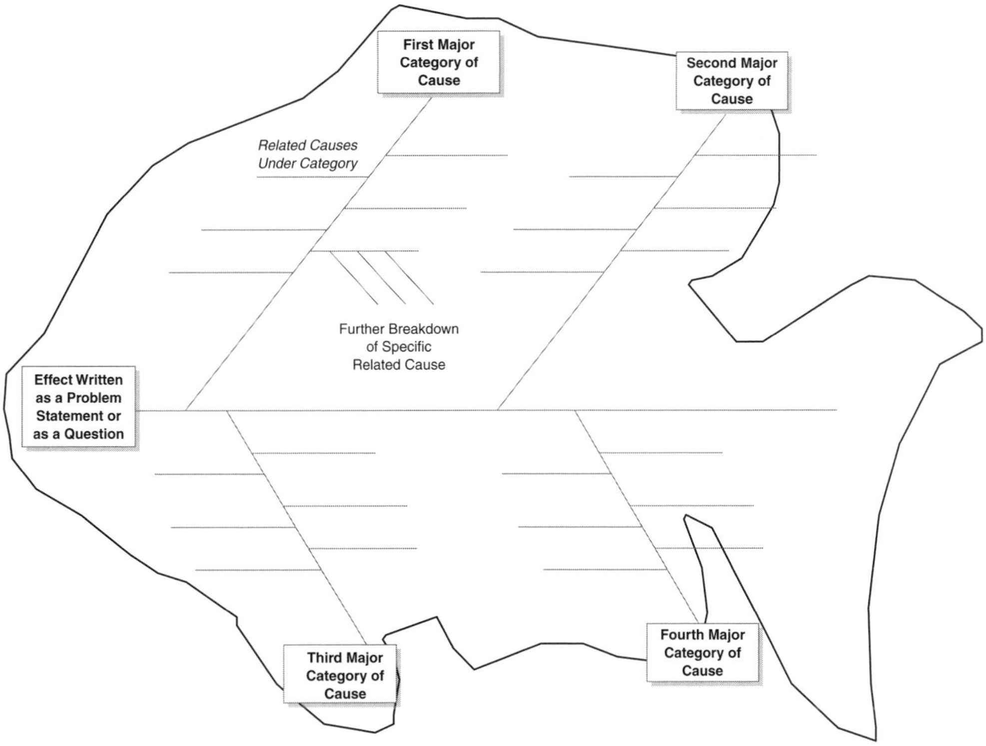

Source: Dianne Kinnison.

Figure 7.3 Flow Chart

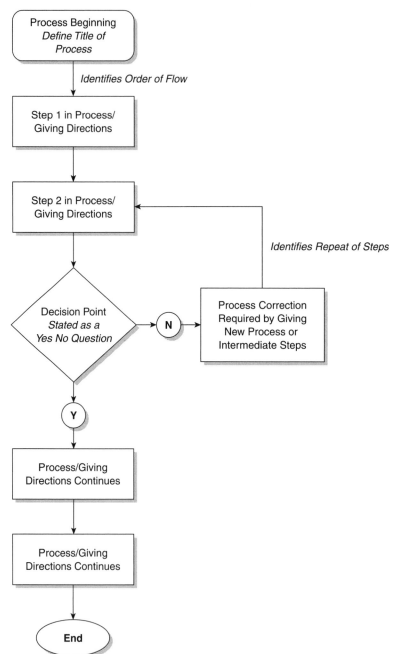

Source: Dianne Kinnison.

Final Thoughts on Using Visuals and Technology

The best technology available today exists to *assist* teachers in some way. The teacher who relies on the overhead projector and is rooted to a spot not far from the projector itself while speaking incessantly in a darkened room is asking for trouble. The same can be said of the use of electronic slide shows or interactive whiteboards. Even the most sophisticated technology should not and cannot replace the classroom teacher.

In Chapter 8 we'll explore the world of storytelling as a powerful tool in the active classroom. Kids and adults of any age love a good story, and we'll explore ways to open the doors to content with stories.

8

Unlocking Doors
With Storytelling

My favorite history professor had a gold pocket watch on a chain. When he removed that watch from his vest pocket and placed it in the corner of the large black desk in front of the classroom, we all sat back and relaxed in pleasurable anticipation of the story we knew was imminent. He had the ability to tell wonderful stories that transported us back to the Great Britain of another time. Kings and queens, prime ministers, philosophers, and other luminaries—and perhaps less well-known inhabitants—came to life through the power of his stories. He used them to engage us and unlock doors into our imagination. When he finished, we had questions, and he asked a good many of his own in order to flesh out the historical facts and concepts that formed the foundation for the story. He used the stories to unlock the doors to the facts, events, and other content that formed the substance of the course.

As a child I spent a good deal of time outside, playing with all the other kids in the neighborhood a rather low-tech and extremely physical game called "kick the can" by its practitioners. One of us "guarded" the can while everyone else tried to be the first to kick the can without being tagged by the kid guarding it. There were other games (red rover come over, four-square) that gave us plenty of opportunities to dirty our clothes and bring ourselves to a relative state of exhaustion in the process. The black and white television in our living room went unused for most of the day and evening during the summer and on weekends. The on-and-off knob and channel selector were both controlled by my grandparents, with whom I lived. I got tons of exercise during the day, and I watched little television in the evening. My grandmother read to me every night, and so my imagination got quite a workout before I went to sleep.

I don't claim that everyone growing up in the 1950s had this same experience, but there can be no doubt that there is a new reality for children today. Jensen (2007) reports that "the average child is watching media three to five hours per day (20–30 hours per week)" (p. 37). Leaving aside for the moment that time spent looking at a computer or television screen displaces time for play and other beneficial *physical* movement, this passive viewing also preempts "the developmental lack of imagination that demands full sensory, motor, emotional, and human interaction/intercommunication practice" (Hannaford, 2005, p. 75). So how do we get our students' imaginations off the bench and into the game?

Storytelling engages our minds in a way that television simply cannot do. According to Ollerenshaw and Lowery (2006), "[s]torytelling stimulates creative images about the world in the listener's mind. These images engage the listener during the storytelling experience and are interpreted by the listener as the story unfolds" (p. 31). My experience has been that students enjoy listening to stories, and that this is the first step to getting them engaged. The second step is to convince them that they are capable of telling stories themselves and, by so doing, develop their own communication skills.

Marzano (2007) reminds us that students like to talk about themselves, and "[o]ne simple technique for engaging students and enhancing their level of energy is to create situations that allow them to talk about their interests" (p. 114). Glazer (2006) gives teachers a way to accomplish that by having students bring to school collections of objects they may have (baseball cards, stamps, stones, photos, etc.). The purpose is to get students to use their objects or collections as props as they talk about them. To get the ball rolling, teachers can begin with a very informal discussion on something they collect and, obviously, value highly. This provides a model for subsequent discussions and keeps it very informal. The idea is to "guide the children to understand that an object can represent an entire story" (p. 86).

After doing this for a month or so, Glazer suggests moving from objects to words as the basis for student storytelling. The words (related to science, math, or any other subject) should "represent an event, theme, idea, or an object that facilitates storytelling" (p. 87). Once the words are chosen and placed in a box:

1. students are paired;

2. each partner selects a card from the box, without looking;

3. students look at their words and share their stories (based on the word) with their partner;

4. after telling the stories, students write them down (or draw them, or both); and

5. students then use the selected word as the title and explain to the class why the story and its title are appropriately matched. (p. 87)

The object, of course, is to build the communication skills and confidence of the students. Beginning, in this case, with something familiar (their own collection of objects) and moving eventually to subject-area content (words related to that content) ensures that students don't have to tackle difficult content information before mastering the processes involved.

Storytelling can be used "as an advance organizer, beginning your lessons or units with storytelling to engage students; storytelling serves to inform students about the purpose of the upcoming activity or concept, prompts questions, sparks thinking about the concept, and triggers connections with prior experiences" (Ollerenshaw and Lowery, 2006, p. 34). Once students are engaged in this manner, teachers can move into more unfamiliar and therefore more difficult material. In working with seventh graders on the U.S. Civil War, I approached the topic of abolitionism in the 1850s through a story from my own early adolescence.

First, I gave my students a short geography lesson that included the drawing in Figure 8.1.

Figure 8.1 Map 1

Source: Brian T. Jones

I wanted them to visually understand how western Pennsylvania sits between Lake Erie and modern-day West Virginia. I also wanted to remind them that Canada is not too far across Lake Erie from my hometown of North East, a few miles east of Erie, Pennsylvania. Finally, I added eastern Ohio and southwestern New York to the drawing, along with the city of Pittsburgh. This whole "geography lesson" did not take more than a couple of minutes. To give them more time to digest the information, I would ask if there was anyone in the classroom from Pennsylvania, Ohio, New York, or West Virginia. There was always someone who had lived in one of those states and it gave those students a close personal connection to the discussion.

Second, since our topic was the late antebellum period of U.S. history, I introduced a bit of historical context by pointing out that West Virginia was not a state prior to the Civil War. By explaining that what is now West Virginia was western Virginia in the 1850s, and by adding that Virginia was a slave state and Pennsylvania was a free state, I was able to begin shifting the students from the present day into that decade just prior to the Civil War. I pointed out that, because slavery did not exist in Canada, many runaway slaves sought help in getting there.

Figure 8.2 Map 2

Source: Brian T. Jones

Having delivered a very short geography lesson (based on the visual in Figure 8.1), and having followed that up with some historical context from the Antebellum Period related to the places on the map, I then told them the following true story.

One of the oldest houses in North East (see Figure 8.1) was across the street from where I lived. When I was in the sixth grade, a friend and I often played together in the house, which belonged to his grandmother. In the front foyer of the house was a trap door which led down into a short hallway opening into a secret room that contained two dirt benches with a dirt table in between the benches. Each of these benches was wide enough to seat two people, but there was not room to stand. Using a flashlight, we discovered an old lantern, a checkerboard (with checkers), and some wooden utensils, among other artifacts.

I can relate with utter certainty that I had the students' attention at this point. When I asked if anyone had questions, *they always did*. It took a combination of the map, some historical context, and the story to open the door to a deep and satisfying discussion of what that house was in the period before the Civil War: a station on the Underground Railroad. This allowed me to work into subsequent conversations the Compromise of 1850, the Fugitive Slave Law, Harriet Tubman, "Bloody" Kansas, Dred Scott, John Brown, and other people and events that were part of any discussion of the United States in the 1850s.

Earlier in my career as a social studies teacher, I used lecture and the overhead projector to uncover the sequence of laws and events that led to the breakout of war in 1861. I have no doubt that, in spite of my best efforts, I did not get my students very deeply involved in the material. On the other hand, when I first used the story of the Underground Railroad station in 1993, I was able to engage my middle school students and keep them engaged *because the moment they started asking questions, they invested in the outcome and wanted to know more*. The difference was illuminating, and once again I was reminded of the power of storytelling first-hand.

Since that time I have used the story with students and adults alike, and I have made a few modifications. First, at the point where I used to ask for questions (after telling the story), I now ask participants to turn to a neighbor and discuss questions they would like to ask *if they could ask questions of me*. After a couple of minutes, I record several of the questions on the board or chart *without actually answering the questions at that point*.

Here are some questions frequently asked by students and adults alike:

- What was the room in the basement used for?
- Why did the fugitives have to hide if Pennsylvania was a "free" state?
- Was the house a station on the Underground Railroad?
- Who owned the house in the 1850s?
- Did fugitives cross the lake? Where? When? How? With whom?
- Did the lake freeze in the winter? If so, could it be crossed?
- Were fugitive slaves finally free in Canada?

As stated earlier, when they begin to ask questions and discuss them with each other, the students are investing heavily in the eventual outcome, which is not only "what happened" in the story, but an understanding of the Underground Railroad, the Fugitive Slave Law, and much else related to the institution of slavery and the coming of the Civil War. When I start with the geography lesson (Figure 8.1), the material still belongs to me. The historical context (Figure 8.2) is mine. *By the time they ask questions and finish the story, they "own" the material.* This transfer of ownership from me to them is important because, with their interest piqued, I can now move into the content, safe in the knowledge that everyone in the room is along for the ride.

Nathanson (2006), after reviewing the research on its effect on teaching and learning, begins by saying that "[s]tory, or narrative, is a powerful—perhaps the most powerful—tool for teaching and learning because of its ability to hook audiences, activate the pleasure principle, and facilitate retention" (p. 2). He concludes that "Recognizing the power of story and using it in the classroom gives teachers an effective teaching tool to promote active learning" (Nathanson, p. 20). That "hook" can serve to get students engaged in most subject-area content.

Some teachers will use a stool or captain's chair each time they tell a story, and the fact that the stool or chair is in the room that day signals to the students that, at some point, the teacher is going to do just that. I find it helpful when beginning a story to pause for a moment and look at the ceiling or off to the side. This pause, I believe, gives students time to adjust to what is coming and builds anticipation. Lipman (1999) says that in normal conversation, a pause would invite the listener to reply or add to the conversation. An intentional pause during a story, however, "creates a powerful silence that may elicit eagerness, dread, or laughter" (p. 35).

An extended pause at a crucial point in the story can serve as an opportunity for the teacher/storyteller to invite students to turn to a partner and predict what they think happens next. Once students have shared with a neighbor their own version of the story's outcome, the teacher can then ask a few students to share their theories. Then, the teacher begins the story again, repeating the extended pause and student conjecture once more before finishing the story. I have found that the anticipation built in this way at each pause gets students to invest heavily in the story's outcome and any point the teacher is using the story to make. Prediction is a powerful tool, and a story with a sense of mystery is perfect for this use of the mighty pause.

Final Thoughts on Unlocking Doors With Storytelling

Stories used in the classroom may be personal, told by teachers or students, or they may be resources selected as part of the curriculum. Personal stories are usually remembered because of our emotional attachment to them, and because they do not tend to lose their immediacy or effectiveness over time.

Maguire (1998) provides a very good reason for sharing our own stories with others by informing us that "getting involved in developing and telling personal stories keeps us from unfairly dismissing large portions of our lives as boring, routine, or unremarkable" (p. 18). Every student has personal stories, the sharing of which may help build self-confidence—something of value not only in the active classroom but in the workplace. Gewertz (2007) affirms that in the global economy of today, "it is not enough to be academically strong" (p. 1). Oral communication skills are an important part of the workplace equation today. Teachers can help develop those skills by providing opportunities for students to relate their own personal stories. The confidence they build may contribute directly to success in their chosen field.

Chapter 9 will reveal the differences between the expectations of students today as contrasted to those of the baby boomers (my generation). This chapter will also give teachers some lesson plans in the four core subject areas that demonstrate the uses of movement, conversation, graphic organizers (which benefit visual learners a great deal), state changes, and other elements of the active classroom.

9

Considering the New Reality and Practical Applications

Some of my fondest memories come from the occasions when my father, grandfather, and I would go to Cleveland Municipal Stadium to see a baseball game. On a Sunday afternoon in the late 1950s, there might be 50,000 fans in attendance to see a double header between the Cleveland Indians and the New York Yankees. Often, one or two of my friends would accompany us and we would be quite content to watch the game with a scorecard in one hand and a pencil (or hot dog) in the other. Within a couple of innings, my dad had met and made the acquaintance of everyone around us in the stands, talking about which pitcher had his "stuff" today and which batter's average had fallen off lately. Such musical entertainment as was on offer was provided by an organist somewhere in the vast stadium. Between innings, we talked and compared scorecards. The ballpark scoreboard and the game itself provided the visuals. Such were our expectations, and we were not disappointed (unless the Yankees beat the Indians).

Almost 50 years later, my wife and I joined friends of ours and attended a game between the Pirates and the Houston Astros in Pittsburgh's beautiful new baseball stadium, PNC Park. The stark difference between my childhood experience at the ballpark and what I encountered five decades later simply underscores how much the expectations of today's kids have been altered. Music of all kinds was playing almost continuously between innings. The massive scoreboard that filled the stands just beyond center field was constantly in use, with replays, videos, pictures and bios of the players, and much else. Images flashed on the screen in much the same way as they do on a television screen—rapidly and constantly. The open space above the centerfield seats provided a simply beautiful view of downtown Pittsburgh, a view that improved even more as the sun went down and we could see the spectacular Pittsburgh skyline lit-up after dark. The old hot dog stands of my youth had been replaced by modern restaurants, and there was a fudge stand not a dozen rows behind me. Every moment was carefully and masterfully choreographed, and every one of our senses was catered to that evening. The Pirates and Astros did play a game that day (and the Pirates won), but in those couple of hours I realized how much had changed. That stadium had been built not just for baseball, but for the fans of this generation. It was a visual and auditory feast. Those who built it had thought of everything, and in doing so had tipped their hat to the new reality—that the kids and young adults of today expect so much more than my friends and I did all those years ago.

Anyone who has watched even a small amount of television today will instantly pick up on the new reality. Images on the screen change at such speeds that someone who grew up in the 50s and 60s can only stare in wonder. Television and movie screens often display multiple images, each of them changing so quickly it is impossible to keep up or concentrate. Movies often seem to be a collection of action sequences tied together loosely by a story line that has to be explained in short and very occasional breaks in the action. I often have a difficult time telling what is real and what is computer-generated imagery. For adults of a certain age, the mind, as they say, *boggles*. This generation wouldn't have it any other way. This is the new reality, and the kids bring that reality with them into our classrooms.

All this brings new challenges for teachers trying to manage process and keep the momentum going in today's classroom. The teacher who lectures twenty-four/seven will frustrate students whose expectations go way beyond listening to the teacher talk for a fifty-five-minute period or a ninety-minute block. As we have seen, students can sit still and listen to lecture for only a few minutes before their minds wander and they disconnect.

In the choreography of planning, then, teachers need to take into account that students need to do something different every few minutes. In so doing, a teacher is "changing the 'state' of the audience. The word *state* in this situation refers to the audience's physiology, their physical and mental state" (Allen, 2002, p. 33). A teacher who changes the physical or mental state of her students has affected a state change. For kids who have been seated, standing qualifies as a physical state change. The introduction of music into the lesson would qualify as a mental state change.

Jensen (2005a) considers what it means to "manage states" in the classroom. Teachers need to consider carefully what state the kids are in before asking them to take part in something new. It is necessary, according to Jensen, to ask the following question before introducing a new activity: "Is the state I am seeing appropriate for the next action (target behavior) I want?" (p. 109). For example, if students have been sitting for several minutes, having them stand, stretch, and walk a bit before asking them to find a conversation partner somewhere in the room may make them more willing to participate. Teachers need to invest in the constant reading of students' states as a way to determine when and how a state change can be best accomplished (Jensen, p. 109).

The new reality for kids demands that teachers take a close look at the old lesson plans and the old methodology. The *content* in the average language arts or economics classroom may not have changed substantially over the years, but what is needed to manage process and keep students engaged certainly has. Just as those who create new ballparks around the country pay attention to the needs of the fans, teachers need to acknowledge where kids are in terms of their expectations.

In Chapter 6 ("Teaching to All Modalities"), we looked at making sure everyone's learning preferences are taken into account in the lesson-planning stage. As teachers design lessons, making sure changes follow fairly swiftly one on the other will help to keep students engaged. On the next few pages, we share sample lesson plans that model some of the strategies included in this book. For example, the first lesson plan for middle school language arts instruction incorporates movement, conversation, a mini-lecture, and music (while students are up and sharing).

Two of the four lesson plans—language arts and science—are intended for shorter middle school class periods (fifty-five minutes), and the others have been created for high school blocks of ninety minutes. Notice that each follows a similar format: objectives, materials, procedure, and assessment.

Figure 9.1   Middle School Language Arts Lesson Plan (55-minute class period)

(Developed by Karen O'Meara)

Unit: Elements of the Short Story

Lesson: Point of View in the Short Story

I. Lesson Objectives: By the end of the lesson, students will:

  a. identify the point of view in a short story;

  b. understand the following literary terms: Narration, First Person, Omniscient, Limited Omniscient;

  c. interact with classmates to share opinions and generate ideas; and

  d. rewrite a classic short story from a different point of view.

II. Lesson Materials/Supplies:

  a. Student copies of the short stories "The Ransom of Red Chief" and "The Gift of the Magi," by O. Henry

  b. Book, *The True Story of the Three Little Pigs,* by Jon Scieszka

  c. Whiteboard, markers, pencil, paper

  d. Music player with selected songs

III. Lesson Procedure/Content:

  a. Teacher lectures on narration, one of the elements of a short story, explaining three points of view when a writer tells his story.

    i. First Person (personal): The main character tells the story ("I")

    ii. Omniscient (impersonal, third person): The story is told from the viewpoint of someone who knows the thoughts and feelings of all of the characters.

    iii. Limited Omniscient (third person): The author limits what he tells the reader to what a single character could observe or know.

  b. Students meet in groups of four (intentional grouping) to read the short story, "The Ransom of Red Chief" by O. Henry.

  c. Discussion Activity: Think-Pair-Share

    i. Students are given think time to ponder the posted questions (whiteboard): "Who is telling the story?" "How do you know who the narrator is?" "Which point of view is used to tell this story?" "How might the story change if told from a different point of view?"

    ii. Students mill around the room to music and find a partner when the music stops. They discuss the questions for two minutes, thank each other for sharing, and return to their seats.

  d. Students share aloud the point of view used in "The Ransom of Red Chief," by O. Henry. (First Person)

  e. Students meet in new groups of four (intentional grouping) to read the short story, "The Gift of the Magi," by O. Henry.

  f. Discussion Activity: Think-Pair-Share

    i. Students are given think time to ponder the same four posted questions for this story.

    ii. Follow previously stated directions for student discussions (III. c. ii)

  g. Students share aloud the point of view used in "The Gift of the Magi," by O. Henry. (Omniscient)

(Continued)

Figure 9.1 *(Continued)*

h. Activity: Think-Write-Pair-Share

   i. Students think of a time when someone was worried about them and write a brief paragraph about the incident from their point of view (First Person). They rewrite the same paragraph in third person sharing only the worried person's perspective of the incident. (Limited Omniscient)

   ii. Students mill around the room to music, pair with a different student, and share paragraphs with each other.

i. Teacher reads aloud *The True Story of the Three Little Pigs,* by Jon Scieszka (told from the wolf's point of view).

IV. Lesson Evaluation (Assessment)

a. Students think of other short stories that could be written from a different point of view.

b. They meet with a partner to generate a list of stories. (Example: *Cinderella* as told from the stepmother or prince's point of view)

c. Students select one story and rewrite it from a different point of view.

Figure 9.2   Middle School Science Lesson Plan (55-minute class period)

Developed by Jenny Sue Flannagan

Unit: **Matter**

Lesson: Heat and States of Matter

I. Lesson Objectives: By the end of the lesson, students will:

   a. design an investigation to determine the effect of heat on the state of matter; and

   b. record the information they collect, make measurements, and graph.

II. Lesson Materials/Supplies:

   a. graduated cylinders

   b. water

   c. beakers

   d. heat source

   e. timer or clock

III. Lesson Procedure/Content:

   a. Teacher begins lesson by using a four-question strategy to guide students to develop the testable question. Teacher begins with question one: How does changing the temperature of water affect how fast it evaporates?

   b. Teacher begins the lesson by asking students to brainstorm on a sheet of paper what they think water can do. In other words, how does it act? Teachers should give students 3 minutes individually, without talking, to come up with a list.

   c. Once 3 minutes is up, have the students stand and work as a team to list those things they know water can do.

   d. Group brainstorming process using Numbered Heads Together (Kagan, 1994, p. 10:2).

      i. Students stand up with the students in their groups.

      ii. Students each share the list they brainstormed.

      iii. When students hear an idea that they did not think of, they write down the idea on their own list

      iv. Once a team is done sharing, they sit down.

      v. Teacher calls a student number, and all the students with that number stand to answer.

      vi. Teacher records ideas on the board or overhead.

   e. Teacher guides students to pick the action of evaporation.

   f. Teacher asks the second question in the four-question strategy model: "If we were going to design an experiment around the action of evaporating water, what materials would we need?"

      i. Again, teacher has students brainstorm individually for 2 minutes.

      ii. Once time is called, group members stand-up, put their heads together, and share their ideas.

      iii. Teacher calls a number and has students share ideas.

      iv. Teacher lists ideas on the board.

   g. Teacher goes over the list of materials just brainstormed by the class. Teacher says, "Is it okay if we use the following materials . . .?" Teacher selects the following materials from list: water and heat source.

(Continued)

Figure 9.2 *(Continued)*

h. Teacher asks the third question in the four-question strategy: "If we are going to design an experiment around evaporating water, what can we change about the water that might affect how it evaporates?"

    i. Students brainstorm individually for 2 minutes.

    ii. Once time is called, group members stand up, put their heads together and share their ideas.

    iii. Teacher calls a number and has students share ideas.

    iv. Teacher lists ideas on the board. Sample ideas might be: change the amount of water; type of water (distilled versus tap); color of water. For the heat source: teacher might change type of heat source (sun versus light inside); having heat and having no heat; time of heat (long time versus short time).

    v. Teacher guides students to decide on having heat present or not having heat.

i. Teacher asks the fourth question in the four-question strategy: "If we are going to design an experiment around evaporating water, and we have a setup where one container of water is placed under a heat source like a lamp and the other is placed somewhere in the room, what could we observe or measure that might indicate that the heat affected the evaporating water?"

    i. Students brainstorm individually for 2 minutes.

    ii. Once time is called, group members stand up, put their heads together, and share their ideas.

    iii. Teacher calls a number and has students share ideas.

    iv. Teacher lists ideas on the board. Sample ideas might be: time it takes to evaporate. Teacher guides students to select measuring the time it takes for the water to evaporate.

j. Teacher then works with students to write the sample testable question: What is the affect of temperature on the time it takes water to evaporate?

k. Teacher then assists students with development of the hypothesis, identification of the variables in the experiment, and development of the data table.

    i. Students conduct experiment and collect data.

l. Once data has been collected, teacher will work with students to calculate the rate of evaporation by dividing the amount of evaporated water by the total time it took to evaporate.

m. Discussion Activity

    i. Students are given think time to ponder the following question posted on the whiteboard: "Did the observations/data collected support your hypothesis?"

    ii. Students are asked to mill around the room to music with their hand up and, when the music stops, find a partner. They discuss the question for two minutes, thank each other for sharing, and return to their seats.

n. Students share aloud whether the data collected supported their hypothesis.

o. Students are given the question "Do you think temperature affects evaporation?"

    i. Students are given think time.

    ii. Students are asked to mill around the room to music with their hand up and, when the music stops, find a partner. They discuss the question for two minutes, thank each other for sharing, and return to their seats.

p. Students share aloud if temperature affects evaporation.

IV. Lesson Evaluation (Assessment)

a. Teacher poses question to students: What changes might occur if you used a substance other than water? How would you go about testing for those changes?

b. Students write their response on a small piece of paper which must be handed to the teacher as an "exit ticket" as the student leaves the room.

Figure 9.3   Secondary Mathematics Lesson (90-minute block)

Developed by Kathleen Dempsey

Unit: Functions

Lesson: Rate of Change

I. **Lesson Objectives:**

  a. Enduring Understanding:

    i. The shape of a graph is determined by rate of change.

    ii. Functions can be used to make predictions.

  b. Essential Questions:

    i. How do differences in the rate of change affect the shape of a graph?

    ii. Why can functions be used to make predictions?

  c. Objectives:

    i. Students will compare and contrast linear, quadratic, and exponential functions using physical models.

    ii. Students will represent functions in multiple ways—table, graph, equation.

    iii. Students will use appropriate mathematical language to communicate their work to peers.

    iv. Students will make predictions using their knowledge of function.

  d. Vocabulary: linear function, nonlinear function, rate of change, independent variable, dependent variable, coordinate grid, x-axis, y-axis

II. **Lesson Materials/Supplies:**

  a. string, scissors, pattern blocks (equilateral triangles only)

  b. grid paper, unlined paper

III. **Lesson Procedure/Content:**

  a. Launch:

  Before introducing the tasks for the lesson, the teacher should display two graphs (one linear and one nonlinear) and ask students to compare and contrast the graphs. The Think-Pair-Share strategy (Kagan, 1994, p. 11:2, originally developed by Professor Frank Lyman and his associates at the University of Maryland Howard County Southern Teacher Education) would be appropriate for this part of the lesson. After pairs have discussed the graphs, the teacher should bring the class together as a whole group to share observations. Encourage the use of mathematical terminology as students discuss. Let the students know that, during the lesson activity, they will investigate the difference between types of functions. Remind students of the essential questions for the session.

  b. Grouping:

  Divide students into groups of 6 students each. Within each group have students count off from 1–3. Students will work in pairs (ones together, twos together, etc.) for the activity.

c. Exploration:
Each pair of students will be assigned a task card that represents one type of function. The students will follow directions on the task card and represent the model with a table of values, a graph, and an equation. When each group has completed the task, the pair will report back to the group of 6 to describe their task and explain their work. As needed, pairs of students may consult with pairs who have the same task. Students will be expected to complete an individual chart showing the table of values, the shape of the graph, and the equation for each task. The class will work with the teacher during the summary to identify the type of function.

Each pair of students must answer the following questions for the assigned task:

  i. Describe the pattern in the model, and create a table of values.

  ii. Graph the table of values on a coordinate grid.

  iii. Predict the 10th stage of the pattern.

  iv. Identify the dependent variable and independent variable in each task.

  v. Write an equation to express the pattern algebraically.

Each group of 6 students should generalize the three tasks by creating a chart in their notebook similar to the one below.

Table of Values

Input (x)	Output (y)	Equation	Sketch of Graph	Type of Function

d. Summary:
When the groups have finished reporting, the teacher should help the students summarize and understand their tasks. Once again students should work with the teacher to compare and contrast the data tables, graphs, and equations. Students should be encouraged to compare the first and second differences of y values in the table as well as the use of exponents in the equation. In this way, the students will note the difference between the exponential task and the quadratic task.

IV. Lesson Evaluation (Assessment)

The following questions may be used to assess student understanding.

a. How does rate of change affect the shape of a graph?

b. Why can functions be used to make predictions?

c. Think back to task #1. If there were 21 pieces of string, how many cuts were made? Describe how you solved this problem.

(Continued)

Figure 9.3 *(Continued)*

Task Cards:

Task #1

Consider that a piece of string is positioned in a "U" shape as shown below:

Build a table of value to determine how many pieces of string result with 1 cut, 2 cuts, 3 cuts, 4 cuts, etc.

- Describe the pattern in the model, and create a table of values.
- Graph the table of values on a coordinate grid.
- Predict the 10th stage of the pattern.
- Identify the dependent variable and independent variable.
- Write an equation to express the pattern algebraically.

Task #2

Use equilateral triangles to build at least 5 stages of larger equilateral triangles. See example below.

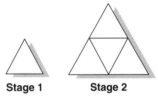

Stage 1   Stage 2

Build a table of values to represent the stage number and the required number of triangles needed to build the figure.

- Describe the pattern in the model, and create a table of values.
- Graph the table of values on a coordinate grid.
- Predict the 10th stage of the pattern.
- Identify the dependent variable and independent variable.
- Write an equation to express the pattern algebraically.

Task #3

Build a table of values that will show the number of sections that result as a piece of paper is folded. For example, fold a piece of paper one time. How many sections result? (2 sections) Fold the paper a second time, how many total sections result in the paper? (4 sections) Record these observations in a table of values.

- Describe the pattern in the model, and create a table of values.
- Graph the table of values on a coordinate grid.
- Predict the 10th stage of the pattern.
- Identify the dependent variable and independent variable in each task.
- Write an equation to express the pattern algebraically.

Lesson adapted from "Using Models to Build an Understanding of Functions" by Kathleen Cramer, *Mathematics Teaching in the Middle School"*, National Council of Teachers of Mathematics, January 2001.

Figure 9.4 United States Government Lesson Plan (90-minute block)

Developed by Lannah Hughes

Unit: **Civil Rights and Civil Liberties (United States Government)**

Lesson: Civil Liberties

I. Lesson Objectives: By the end of the lesson, students will:

  a. describe conflicts between individuals and government in a democratic society; and

  b. analyze conflicting points of view

II. Lesson Materials/Supplies:

  a. Transparency of *Word Splash** terms

  b. One copy per student of the short story "Harrison Bergeron," by Kurt Vonnegut

  c. Class and media center resources on selected Supreme Court cases and laws (see list within lesson procedures)

  d. Chart paper and markers

  e. One copy per student of the exit ticket (see specifics within lesson procedures)

III. Lesson Procedure/Content:

  a. Introducing the Lesson

    i. Instruct students that they will be reading a story entitled "Harrison Bergeron." (Story summary: the year is 2081; society has enacted a multitude of laws to ensure equality. The story centers around George and Hazel as they watch an unfolding news event.)

    ii. Post the rendering of words and phrases that follows (word splash) on the overhead, or give each student a hard copy.

    iii. Students may work in pairs and use the words/phrases as evidence to make predictions about what the story will be about. What connections can students make between and among the words/phrases that are part of the word splash?

Word Splash for "Harrison Bergeron"

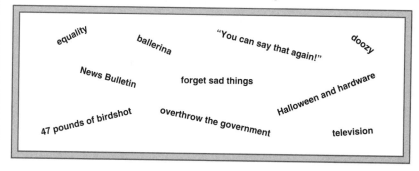

    iv. Allow the students (in their pairs) approximately two to five minutes to write down how they think the words/phrases will be used in the story. In other words, what are they predicting this story will be about? Ask volunteers to share their thoughts with the entire class.

    v. Provide students with copies of the story to read, asking them to check to see if their predictions are correct.

(Continued)

Figure 9.4   *(Continued)*

a. Introducing the Lesson *(continued)*

   vi. Upon completion of the reading, lead students in a discussion using the following questions as examples.

      (a) "There is a point beyond which even justice becomes unjust" (Sophocles). How does this quote relate to the story of Harrison Bergeron?

      (b) Is it possible to definitively define equality?

      (c) Can a government ensure the freedom and equality of the individual citizen?

b. Teaching the Lesson

   i. Divide the class into 10 small teams. Assign each team one of the following topics. Their task is to use classroom and media center resources to research the basic provisions/ruling for their assigned topic. Students should then write their findings on a sheet of chart paper and post around the room.

Sedition Act of 1798	*Schenck v. United States* (1919)
Espionage Act of 1981	*New York Times v. Sullivan* (1964)
Executive Order 9066 (1942)	Smith Act (1943)
Ex Parte Milligan (1866)	Espionage and Sedition Acts (1917–1918)
selected portions of the Patriot Act	*Texas v. Johnson* (1989)

   i. Have each group provide an overview on their topic for the class. After a few of the groups have presented their information, ask all students to take a two minute pause and discuss their interpretations of the information.

   iii. As a whole class, ask students to consider and discuss the balance between the rights of the individual and the needs of government.

IV. Closing the Lesson/Lesson Evaluation

a. Distribute the following exit ticket to students. Students should complete the requested information and return their exit ticket to the teachers before they leave class.

EXIT TICKET

1. What problems can be encountered in a democratic society when the aims of individuals and the government are different?

2. Benjamin Franklin is credited with the following: "They who can give up essential liberty to obtain a little temporary safety deserve neither liberty nor safety" (1775). Do you agree or disagree? Why?

3. Identify three similarities between the events in "Harrison Bergeron" and the events discussed in class today.

---

* Word Splash (originally created by Dr. W. Dorsey Hammond, Professor of Education at Salisbury University, Maryland, who also calls it the Key Word technique) is a pre-reading strategy.

Final Thoughts on the New Reality and Practical Applications

As the lesson plans indicate, being active in the classroom is not restricted to physical movement. Students who are engaged with powerful graphic organizers or involved in conversations with neighbors are active learners. Students have always had difficulty sitting still and being lectured to for long periods of time, but students of today who are caught up in this new reality are even less able to sit passively while their teachers do the work. They need to be actively involved in the process.

In Chapter 10, the final chapter, we'll explore overall planning for the active classroom and look at some potential obstacles that can, if teachers let them, interfere with those plans.

10

Planning for the Active Classroom

Several years ago a friend told me this true story about a kindergartner on the first day of school. Mom waited anxiously for her daughter to come home after that first morning session and finally spotted the school bus coming down the street. As the bus pulled up to the curb, mom headed out the front door to greet her daughter as she disembarked. It quickly became apparent that the little girl was upset in the extreme, with tears running down her cheeks. When mom asked what was wrong, her kindergartner replied, through the sobs, "They made us come home!!"

One wonders how many fifth, seventh, or twelfth graders feel this way at the end of a day of school. After almost four decades in the field of education, my guess is *not many*. A clue as to why this may be true can be found in the following list of things I have observed in classrooms where kids tend to be passive observers:

- **teacher** talking;
- **teacher** asking questions;
- **teacher** moving around the room;

- **teacher** writing on the board;
- **teacher** explaining;
- **teacher** demonstrating;
- **teacher** disciplining students;
- **teacher** exhausted at the end of the day (and possibly contemplating a career move); and
- **kids** sitting in their seats, listening, taking notes, and doing seat work.

Contrast this with what I have observed in active classrooms over the past few years:

- **kids** sharing with a partner;
- **kids** moving;
- **kids** explaining;
- **kids** demonstrating;
- **kids** singing;
- **kids** laughing;
- **kids** writing on the board or on charts;
- **kids** working in cooperative groups; and
- **teachers** facilitating process.

Many of my teacher friends at the high school and elementary school level were amazed that I could enjoy teaching in middle school. I often told them that the trick to being successful in middle school is to channel all that energy. If teachers can't find ways to take advantage of the inclination of kids to move and talk, teaching can be like holding thirty balloons under water all at once. In my early years as a teacher, my classroom looked much like the *first* list above. I took center stage, and the kids were relegated to the wings.

Over my last four years of teaching in junior high and then middle school, my seventh-grade classrooms shifted along a continuum from extremely passive to a good deal more active. I never achieved the kind of active classroom of the second list, but I have seen those classrooms. I have interviewed teachers and kids in those classrooms. I have talked to the parents of the kids in those classrooms. The difference is amazing, both in student and teacher attitudes and in student performance.

For teachers who have decided to create a classroom that is active, then, there are a few decisions to be made, followed by some considerations for getting started.

I know teachers who have (metaphorically speaking) jumped into the pool with the active classroom concept. Two teachers in particular, Cindy Rickert and Emma Jeter, simply got rid of their student desks and replaced them, with the principal's permission and assistance, with four-person tables placed around the outside perimeter of their classrooms. This opened up the middle of the room for their use of activities that required movement and meeting in pairs and groups. Worksheets became a thing of the past for these two teachers as they helped their students make the successful shift from passive to active learners.

The first decision, then, has to do with whether teachers want to jump into the deep end of the pool, or move more slowly and deliberately down the pool steps and into the shallow end until they get used to the water. Many teachers will make the decision to begin with using music in the classroom, perhaps as the students enter, followed by other strategies later on. Some teachers choose to experiment with their students, having them work in pairs first, followed by larger group work and discussions down the road. Change involves risk and may be difficult for veteran teachers who have become used to set procedures and familiar plans. Moving *slowly*, but *purposefully*, from a program that is fairly passive to one that is increasingly active may make perfect sense.

In either case, but especially if there is going to be a shift from passive to active, building relationships with parents becomes paramount. Parents need to know that procedures and processes in *this* classroom may be different than what they and their kids have become accustomed. Many parents may be skeptical about all the movement, music, and conversation that in all likelihood were not a part of their own educational experience. That initial skepticism on the part of parents will fade, however, as their children show a desire to go to school, begin sharing things that happened in school, and perhaps don't seem to be getting into trouble as frequently.

There is no chapter in this book entitled *Motivating Students*. I agree with W. Edwards Deming (as cited in Jenkins, 1997) that children are born motivated—observe any kindergarten class—and that our job as educators is to "discover what demotivates them, and stop those practices" (p. 27). Therefore, there may be some demotivators, or potential obstacles to learning, that need to be considered carefully when planning for the active classroom. Each obstacle, however, has a possible solution rooted in the concept of an active classroom.

Potential Obstacle: Lack of Classroom Space for Movement
Possible Solution: Move the Furniture Before School Begins

Changing traditional patterns of furniture arrangement will assist teachers in providing sufficient space to meet and hold structured conversations. Moving the teacher's desk to a corner of the room (or simply getting rid of it) will open up "front and center" in the classroom. Using the furniture arrangements (Figures 3.2 and 3.3) in Chapter 3 will go a long way to giving students and teachers room to maneuver and hold frequent conversations. Traditional seating arrangements (Figure 3.1 in Chapter 3) do not allow enough room for classrooms dedicated to being active and interactive.

Potential Obstacle: Inconsistencies in Classroom Leadership
Possible Solution: Demonstrate Consistent Behavior and Establish Consistent Procedures

It has been my experience that a lack of consistency on the part of teachers can result in heaps of confusion, anxiety, and fear. Wong and Wong (2005) inform teachers that time must be spent in the first week of school establishing and practicing procedures until they become routine. "The students must know from day to day how the classroom is structured and organized" (p. 84). Teachers who are going to have students up, moving, and sharing in pairs or groups need to have regular classroom practices clearly understood by students.

Classroom rules (not the same as procedures) should be clearly understood by students from the beginning. Teachers who seem to be making up the rules as the year goes on are headed for trouble down the road. Students need the consistency of knowing what the rules are up front (Wong & Wong, 2005, p. 143). Curwin (2003) suggests that students can help set up rules for the classroom *and for the teacher*. "As with the student rules, you do not have to accept every rule that the students develop" (Curwin, p. 87). Students who have a say in the establishment of the rules may be more likely to feel empowered.

A teacher who has too many rules may find them hard to remember, much less enforce. Smith (2004) recommends five or six at the most. It is also important, as teachers plan, to make certain whatever rules are established "cover the main classroom behaviors and coordinate with school and district policies" (Smith, p. 167).

Regardless of the number of rules or how they are arrived at (with or without student input), consistency in their enforcement throughout the year is one of the keys to success with the group dynamics of the active classroom.

Potential Obstacle: Over-Reliance on Lecture
Possible Solution: Follow a Short Lecture with Processing Time

I enjoy a good lecture. In fact, at any given time I have one or more taped lectures in my car on topics related to history or political science.

I'm an auditory learner, and I spend a good deal of time listening to some of higher education's best lecturers in CD or tape format. But I have an advantage unavailable to most students sitting in a classroom dominated by lecture. If my attention wanders or I need to stop and process information just presented in the taped lecture, I just hit the stop and rewind buttons. If I really don't like the lecture or the lecturer, I simply quit listening altogether and take it back to the library at my earliest opportunity. Students have no such advantage. They are required to attend the class and forced to sit, listen, and take notes for the duration of what *may* be a fifty-five- or ninety-minute lecture.

In classrooms, then, where lecture is the primary method of delivery, students tend to be passive observers. In these teacher-centered classrooms, the teacher is doing the work and students may not be engaged in the process. In active classrooms, students are not "viewed as the vessel to be filled" (Fogarty, 1990, p. ix). A short period (ten minutes, give or take) of lecture might be followed by two or three minutes where students "summarize key points, define particular terms, or make connections between the new material and their own experiences" (Lipton & Wellman, 2000, p. 62).

Potential Obstacle: Breadth vs. Depth of Coverage
Possible Solution: Seek Student Understanding Above All

As a former social studies teacher, I can appreciate the dilemma faced by teachers of United States history. When I first started teaching that subject in the early 1970s, I attempted to cover as much as possible and used the textbook as my guide. I moved through the year at a rapid and dizzying pace, determined to "cover it all" in two semesters. Even after sacrificing depth of understanding for breadth of coverage, I still found it difficult to get beyond World War II. That was *still* the case for me (and a new set of junior high school students) fifteen years later, at which point *fifteen additional years of history had been added to the curriculum.* My students' depth of understanding by any measure was less than satisfactory, and I can only think that for them it was like sitting as a passenger in a speeding train and watching the scenery pass by in an unrecognizable blur.

In planning for the active classroom, teachers need to grapple with the fact that "[m]ost curriculums simply pack too much information into too little time—at a significant cost to the learner" (Brooks & Brooks, 1999, p. 39). Tomlinson and McTighe (2006) remind us that the *what* (curriculum content) is only part of the equation if teachers and students are to experience success in the classroom:

In effective classrooms, teachers consistently attend to at least four elements: whom they teach (students), where they teach (learning environment), what they teach (content), and how they teach (instruction). If teachers lose sight of any one of the elements and cease investing effort in it, the whole fabric of their work is damaged and the quality of learning impaired. (p. 2)

When planning, then, teachers need to look carefully at curricular content, along with accompanying texts and other resources, and determine how to best to deal with the content while increasing understanding on the part of kids. Those kids "need the opportunity to practice and become actively engaged with the new learning in order to understand and retain it" (Gregory & Chapman, 2002, p. xiii).

Potential Obstacle: Too Much Individual Seat Time
Possible Solution: Build in Opportunities for Movement

In Chapter 3 I emphasized that kids need to move and that movement enhances the learning process—a happy coincidence. When planning lessons for the active classroom, teachers should include plenty of opportunities for students to stand, stretch, process information with a partner, do some simple physical exercises, and discuss something other than content-related information in order to get them used to interactive processes. In short, we should get students up, sharing, and moving as much as possible.

Potential Obstacle: Reliance on Summative Assessments
Possible Solution: Provide Frequent Opportunities for Formative Assessment

Feedback comes in many forms, and it is a critical part of the continuous improvement process for students. Ongoing formative classroom assessments "provide continuous feedback about students' strengths and weaknesses" (Burke, 2006, p. 4). If assessments are formative, rather than summative, students can be involved in their own assessments or those of their peers as well (Danielson, 2002). Marzano (2003) reports the results of several studies that "indicate that academic achievement in classes where effective feedback is provided to students is considerably higher than the achievement in classes where it is not" (p. 37).

Students need feedback, and if the only assessment is summative (end-of-chapter, end-of-unit, end-of-grading period), then the teacher, feeling pressure to "cover the curriculum," is likely to move on regardless of the fact that students have not done well on those summative exercises. Formative assessments "monitor students' progress and provide meaningful and immediate feedback as to what students have to do to achieve learning standards" (Burke, 2005, p. xx). Fisher and Frey (2007) recommend checking for understanding at least every 15 minutes. By checking frequently, "if a teacher observes that some students do not grasp a concept, he or she can design a review activity to reinforce the concept or use a different instructional strategy to reteach it" (p. 4).

In the high school science classroom I observed (Chapter 1), students developed portfolios of their work that allowed them to gauge where they were in terms of their progress at any given time. "Portfolios focus on a student's products, process, and progress over time and help students self-assess their work as well as set new goals for themselves" (Burke, 2006, p. 4). Goal setting without adequate provisions for frequent and meaningful feedback is an empty exercise. When planning for the active classroom, teachers need to consider how (and how often) feedback will be given to students. Incorporating frequent opportunities to check for student understanding will inform instruction and allow for necessary changes.

Potential Obstacle: Competition vs. Collaboration
Possible Solution: Decrease Competition and Increase Collaboration

Competition in the classroom may set students against each other at a time when we want them to be working together toward a common goal. If the goal becomes winning, then students see others in the class as competitors and cooperation may become a casualty. Ranking of students has the tendency to destroy the joy of learning as students scramble for the best grades (Jenkins, 1997). Students begin to think of themselves as winners and losers, rather than as partners, and may "come to distrust and resent their peers, since the central lesson of all competition is that other people are obstacles to their own success" (Kohn, 1999, p. 38). If learning becomes a zero-sum game, all students will become losers, and the object should be to create as many winners as possible.

Di Giulio (2007) recommends that cooperation and collaboration become the norm in classrooms. "Specifically, this means planning and carrying out cooperative learning practices in the classroom by having students work in pairs and in small groups for at least half their time in school" (p. 26). Learning to work in groups and cooperate with one another would seem to be the best route to work on the kinds of collaborative skills students will need later on in college or in the workplace.

Potential Obstacle: Playing the Blame Game
Possible Solution: Don't Let External Problems Short Circuit Success

Teachers need to avoid taking part in that great educational pastime of blaming everything and everyone else for not being able to move forward on behalf of kids. Jenkins (2003) says, "[i]f blame could improve schooling, American K–12 education would be the envy of the world" (p. xxv). In his book on instructional coaching, Knight (2007) says that among the tough questions we need to ask about schools and the prevailing culture is "Are our teachers focused on becoming better teachers or are they focused on making excuses?" (p. 209). According to Jenkins (2003), there are at least three important difficulties associated with playing the blame game:

1. It does not fix anything;

2. Those in charge can escape responsibility; and

3. It stops educators from searching for underlying causes. (p. xxvi)

If the convenience of being able to lay blame causes us to march in place and avoid necessary improvements and innovations, then we need to remove that barrier and move forward. Getting involved in negative conversations of any sort, I have discovered, serves no real purpose and tends to encourage a culture of negativity in the building and in the classroom.

Potential Obstacle: Classroom Negativity
Possible Solution: Make the Classroom a Safe and Positive Place

Teachers need to make it clear to students that sarcasm, inappropriate behavior, and generally negative attitudes will not be allowed to harm the necessary relationships that are a critical part of creating a family atmosphere in the classroom. Teachers should work hard to build relationships with students, peers, administrators, and parents. Whitaker (2004) points out that "[t]he teacher who sets a positive tone can influence the interactions of everyone in the school" (p. 51). Every classroom will be either a positive or negative environment for students, depending in the first instance on what kinds of relationships teachers build. Gordon (2006) reminds us that "highly talented teachers at all levels spontaneously create positive, supportive classroom environments" (p. 158).

This means that teachers should spend every waking moment before school begins on any given day getting themselves in a positive mood, no matter what happened the night before. As a middle and high school teacher, my first order of business on arriving each morning was to turn on the music and play several of my very favorite songs—tunes calculated to put me in a great frame of mind by the time students began to arrive. Teachers need to put a great deal of thought into what kind of place their classrooms will be.

Potential Obstacle: Insular Teaching vs. Collegiality
Possible Solution: Make Every Effort to Observe Other Teachers and to Be Observed

Teaching can be a lonely profession. Many teachers spend much of their careers in the same building and classroom. Even though great things are going on all around them, many teachers simply do not see it happening. Lezotte (1992) observes that "educators spend less time than members of any other profession in observing the practices of colleagues" (p. 14). The thrust of this book is that students should become active participants in their own learning through conversation, cooperation, and collaboration. The irony, according to Garmston and Wellman (1999), is that "in many schools, professionals who are charged with preparing students to be successful collaborative citizens are themselves cut off from the rich resources offered by true collegiality" (p. 61).

The stakes are simply too high for educators to close their classroom doors and do what they have always done. Improvement requires change, and change is not always easy or convenient, but it is inevitable if we are going to move forward in the continuous improvement process. The good news is that there are, as Conzemius and O'Neill (2006) remind us, schools where teachers and administrators "are courageously confronting whether they have both the skill and the will to make significant changes in their curricular, instructional, and assessment practices" (p. 193). Kaufeldt (2005) affirms that a great teacher is an innovator and "one who continuously adapts to student needs and situations" (p. 1).

Once the need for reflection, innovation, and improvement is accepted, school leaders need to provide time for teachers to observe best practices and then meet to discuss *how* they do what they do and how *what* they do can be made better. Observing and then sharing what is successful should be a part of every school's commitment to continuous improvement, as reflected in their overall professional development plan.

Final Thoughts on Planning for the Active Classroom

One thing that powerful and effective teachers have in common is that they sweep away obstacles and remove barriers that can all too often serve as excuses for not getting the job done. They move inexorably forward and take no prisoners. My most effective teachers and professors over the years were those who were consistent, positive, fair, relentless, and *loved being with us every day*. They were willing to admit mistakes and had a sense of humor that underlined both their humanity and their sense of being human.

I often talk about my favorite teachers. In every case, when I recall my best teachers, they were the one who told stories, and they had us tell *our* stories . . . and when I tell *their* stories, I remember every detail of the rooms in which they taught. I remember where I sat. I have total recall of the myriad ways in which they demonstrated their mastery of the profession. There was, in the final analysis, *something in them* that saw *something in us,* and this intangible, but very real, trait is one that characterizes great teachers through the ages.

In planning for the active classroom, teachers need to remember that kids gotta move and kids gotta talk. More than ever, we as teachers need to provide structured opportunities for them to do both. The new reality of the 21st century is that many of the jobs these students will hold require teamwork, interaction, conversation, and collaboration. Students who spend a good deal of time watching a screen of one size or another need also to be involved in structured conversations in our classrooms. It is necessary for them to learn how to speak with confidence and *listen* with respect and understanding.

Students need to grasp that while there is a place for competition in life, learning to cooperate will open more doors as they enter the workforce and adulthood. "It is time for cooperative learning, where everyone, including the teacher is constantly open to new possibilities" (Hannaford, 2005, p. 234). The active classroom is a veritable hotbed of possibilities for students and teachers alike.

And it's more fun.

Appendix A

The Active Classroom at a Glance

It is my contention that teachers can benefit from observing other classrooms on a regular basis as part of an individual continuous improvement process. In our own classrooms, we are so busy that we don't, or can't, stop to take a good long look at our processes and see the entire experience through the eyes of our students. Sitting *with the students* in someone else's classroom allows teachers to spend time observing closely every aspect of the classroom environment. It also permits the observing teacher to *concentrate on the students themselves* in order to gauge the impact of the lesson. By taking the time to have a thirty-minute teacher-to-teacher conversation at some point after the observation, both teachers benefit from the exercise.

My suggestion is that teachers make arrangements to observe teachers regardless of the content. The tendency is for teachers to observe those who teach the same subject, and that is certainly helpful if one is *concentrating* on content. In considering the active classroom principles (movement, student-to-student conversation, use of music, process-management techniques, etc.), it is not necessary to limit these observations to the classrooms of teachers who teach the same subject. In fact, if one is looking at *process-related areas*, an argument might be made that a science teacher observing another science teacher might get caught up in the familiar *content* and neglect to look at *process*.

The purpose of this appendix, then, is to give teachers (and administrators) some "look fors" and thoughtful questions to consider when observing another classroom. In each of eight areas, corresponding to the material in the first seven chapters of this book, we'll ask observing teachers to ponder the major differences between classrooms that are passive in nature and those that are more active.

In observing other classrooms, then, teachers can look for observational evidence of:

- a safe classroom (Chapter 1);
- purposeful arrangement of furniture and space in the classroom (Chapter 2);
- a collaborative environment (Chapter 2);
- frequency of movement as part of the classroom experience (Chapter 3);
- utilization of music to manage process (Chapter 4);
- confidence and effectiveness of the teacher as presenter (Chapter 5);
- an effective use of visuals and technology (Chapter 7); and
- a commitment to students with different learning styles (Chapter 6).

Each of the eight pages in this appendix will begin with a chart that contrasts active classrooms with those that may be more traditionally passive. This chart will be followed by some questions teachers might try to answer during the observation, along with suggestions for the incorporation of active-classroom principles and strategies in their own classrooms. My hope is that administrators will provide as many opportunities as possible for teachers to get into classrooms and the time to meet with those colleagues about the advantages of involving students in their own learning every day and in every classroom.

Classroom Observation Consideration #1	
Observational evidence of a safe classroom	
The foundation of success in any classroom, passive or otherwise, in our educational system is an environment in which students feel safe, both physically and emotionally. Before taking risks, which is a critical part of the learning process, students must feel they can do so free of ridicule and sarcasm. The only consequence of failure should be improvement.	In an active classroom where students are sharing frequently, collaborating regularly, and otherwise taking risks on a daily basis, a safe environment is absolutely essential. While hiding in a passive classroom may be relatively easy, staying in the background in an active classroom is virtually impossible. Safety is a prerequisite to success.

In the classroom you are observing . . .

Does it appear that students are willing to involve themselves actively in the learning process? Do students appear to feel generally comfortable with interactions? Do they feel free to ask questions?

. . . and your own classroom . . .

Spend adequate time at the beginning of the school year on relationship-building in your classroom. Making frequent deposits in the "relationship bank" will pay off over time. As discussed in Chapter 1, practice basic classroom procedures until everyone in the classroom understands exactly how things are done on a daily basis. Commit to staying calm in the face of behavioral issues that might otherwise disrupt process flow and possibly destroy the very relationships you have worked hard to build. Remember that you teach people, not content.

Observation Notes

Classroom Observation Consideration #2	
Observational evidence of the purposeful arrangement of furniture and space	
In traditional classrooms, the furniture, as we saw in Chapter 3, may be arranged to facilitate cleaning, not learning.	In active classrooms, the furniture has been arranged purposefully by the teacher, with movement and collaboration in mind.

In the classroom you are observing . . .

Take a moment to look around the classroom. What percentage of the space is devoted to student desks and chairs? What percentage is available for students to meet comfortably and efficiently in pairs or groups? Is the arrangement conducive to movement on the part of the teacher as he or she interacts with students?

Figures 3.1, 3.2, and 3.3 from Chapter 3 show three room configurations. Which of these three best describes the room you are visiting?

Figure 3.1   **Figure 3.2**   **Figure 3.3**

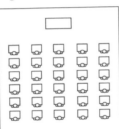

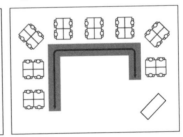

Source: Brian T. Jones, used by permission of Frederic H. Jones & Associates, Inc.

. . . and your own classroom . . .

Remember, your goal in the active classroom is to facilitate movement and conversation between and among students. Experimenting with the positioning of the furniture will help you find just the right arrangement. Student chairs that are welded to the desks may present problems forcing you to become creative about how to accommodate frequent movement and facilitate student-to-student conversations.

Observation Notes

Classroom Observation Consideration #3 Observational evidence of a collaborative environment	
Students in more passive classrooms, especially at the secondary level, may spend a good deal of time seated, listening to the teacher, and taking notes. Seat work may be done alone, rather than with a partner. Reflecting on the content may be something students are expected to do on their own and at home.	In more active classrooms, students are engaged in any number of obvious ways in hands-on and minds-on learning. Time is built into the day or class period for the specific purpose of having students process information in such a way that they can make sense of it, building on knowledge they already brought to the table.

In the classroom you are observing . . .

Is the furniture arranged for easy collaboration, either seated or standing? Does the teacher provide time for pairs or small groups of students to reflect on information that has been presented via direct instruction? If time is not provided for structured conversations, do you see occasions during the lesson where this might have been done?

. . . and your own classroom . . .

Many teachers will take the time to discover the talents and strengths of the students so that deliberate pairings later on will prove beneficial. For example, if Yolanda (an "idea person"), Randy (the "analysis person"), and Fred (who has a reputation for "getting it done") can be placed on the same team for a large project requiring multiple talents, so much the better. Purposeful pairings or groupings will result in harnessing *individual strengths in pursuit of a collaborative goal.*

Before grouping students, spend quality time working on collaborative skills. If "reporter" or "recorder" or "timer" are jobs within the groups, make certain everyone understands *exactly* what those jobs entail. Build in time to practice, practice, and then practice some more before introducing content into the mix.

Observation Notes

Classroom Observation Consideration #4	
Evidence of frequency of movement as part of the classroom experience	
In more traditional classrooms where seat work is the norm and collaboration is rare, life can become one-dimensional and boring. Teachers who do most of the work (and most of the moving) in the classroom may also be doing most of the learning.	Teachers in active classrooms understand that movement facilitates memory and learning, and it provides much-needed breaks on occasion for students who find it difficult to stay seated for long periods of time.

In the classroom you are observing . . .

Are students seated for most of the class period? Are there opportunities for students to stand and reflect on course content with a partner or in a group? Are there obstacles to movement in the classroom? Do the students seem comfortable working in pairs and groups? Do students seem to appreciate the opportunity to stand and move?

. . . and your own classroom . . .

When planning how to work movement into your own classroom environment, consider moving from pairs to trios to quartets in a progression that lets students find comfort and success at each level before moving on. Once students are in their pairs or groups, move among them, listening to what is being said. Remember: Before introducing content into their conversations, have them discuss something totally familiar to them. Once they get the process down, shift them into subject-area conversations. Finally, during longer periods of direct instruction (at their desks), give your kids plenty of "brain breaks" where they can stand, talk, laugh, and generally recharge their batteries before returning to their seats. One teacher who does this frequently reports that she has few discipline problems, partly because she allows for these purposeful breaks and movement in the classroom.

Observation Notes

Classroom Observation Consideration #5 Observational evidence of the utilization of music to manage process	
In traditional classrooms, music may be used infrequently and in support of the content. A social studies teacher, for example, might use songs of the Civil War to enhance students' understanding of that period. That same teacher, later in the school year, may use the song "Over There" during a study of World War I.	Today we have a much greater understanding of the uses of music in the classroom. It can be played as students enter or as they leave; it can be used as a "pad" behind structured conversation; or it can serve as a cue for cleaning up after a lab or getting ready to leave for the next class or for the day.

In the classroom you are observing . . .

Is music being used in any way? If so, how are the kids responding to its use? Is its use tied to *content* (60s music used to enhance students' understanding of that decade in U. S. history) or to *process* (music used to cue a lab cleanup)? As the lesson unfolds, do *you* see opportunities for the use of music along the lines of what we discovered in Chapter 4? If music is used, how do the students respond to its use?

. . . and your own classroom . . .

Many teachers who wish to begin slowly with the introduction of active-classroom strategies into classroom practice begin with music. One of the simplest ways to introduce its use is by playing some upbeat songs as the students enter. A CD player with a remote is probably all you will need.

If students ask you to use their music, my suggestion is that you check it out before playing it in class. Many lyrics are explicit and totally inappropriate for classroom use. My suggestion is that you stick with music from the 60s and 70s, most of which is familiar because of its use in movies, commercials, and television shows.

Observation Notes

Classroom Observation Consideration #6	
Observational evidence of confidence and effectiveness of the teacher as presenter	
Traditional classrooms are replete with teacher-talk in the form of direct instruction. Teachers can get so used to talking that they forget about the effectiveness of the delivery and neglect presentation components such as vocal variety, pitch, timing, use of silence, body language, and the effective use of visuals and technology as part of the presentation. A teacher who talks in a monotone will reduce the effectiveness of the delivery.	In the active classroom, teachers consider all the components of an effective presentation. They may also, as I suggested in Chapter 5, tape themselves in action and get critical visual and auditory feedback that will assist in their own continuous improvement efforts. They may also ask for feedback from their own students in a way that not only helps to the teachers but lets students know they are working on making themselves more effective presenters.

In the classroom you are observing . . .

Are there any indications the teacher is moving too quickly in the direction of information overload? Does the teacher seem to consciously work on her pitch, volume, and timing? Does the teacher allow sufficient wait time after asking a question to allow students to really think about possible answers? Are there occasions when the teacher you are observing uses a purposeful pause to generate thinking or solicit more questions?

. . . and your own classroom . . .

Costa (2008), citing the work of Mary Budd Rowe, recommends at least three seconds of wait time after asking a question. As noted in Costa (p. 210), this increase in wait time can lead to longer student responses, an increase in "the number of unsolicited but appropriate" responses, a decrease in failures to respond, and an increase in student-to-student interaction. When possible, try asking questions that are more open-ended and that lead to more thoughtful deliberation on the part of your students.

Observation Notes

Classroom Observation Consideration #7	
Observational evidence of the effective use of visuals and technology	
In passive classrooms students *may* watch lots of videos. A movie may run for three consecutive days. Before beginning a classroom activity, directions may be given verbally and in a rush, so that students simply wind up asking a dozen questions, chief among which is this classic query: "What are we supposed to be doing?"	Active-classroom teachers don't have time to show an entire movie. They may show short clips that support a concept or other course content. As for directions, they are given one at a time and are posted in clear sight so that students involved in an activity can check visually for the next step in the process.

In the classroom you are observing . . .

As you observe in this classroom, what do you notice about the way directions are given? Are they verbal, or are written directions posted on the board or overhead? If there are posters or other visuals on the walls, is there evidence that they are part of reflective exercises that aid students in processing information and building new knowledge?

. . . and your own classroom . . .

Remember that anytime you can provide a visual backup to a verbal direction, or series of directions, do it. As you plan for a week-long unit in science (for example), have students chart information as part of reflective activities. *Post the charts and leave them up all week long, referring to them as needed.* The charts will provide visual anchors as students wrestle with the material.

Short film clips may be quite enough to highlight a concept, reinforce a point, or otherwise illuminate subject matter. Time is, as every teacher knows, perhaps *the* most precious commodity. Use it wisely and efficiently when it comes to technology.

Observation Notes

Classroom Observation Consideration #8	
Observational evidence of a commitment to students with different learning styles	
Teachers who are high auditory may rely on lecture as the main method of delivery in the traditional classroom. I can attest to that, as I am high auditory and did not think twice about adopting lecture as my single most-used tool. Kids who are high visual or high kinesthetic, as we saw in Chapter 6, do not do well in high-auditory environments.	Teachers in active classrooms understand that we must provide lessons and strategies that engage all learning styles. Increasing the number of visuals and allowing for plenty of movement and hands-on activities will go a long way toward meeting the needs of those who learn and process information differently from high auditory learners.

In the classroom you are observing . . .

Who, in your opinion, seems to be doing the most work—teacher or students? To what extent are the students involved in their own learning? Are students provided with an opportunity to reflect and process information in the classroom? What does the body language of the students say if there are extended periods of lecture in the classroom? Does it appear that the teacher is differentiating by acknowledging various learning styles?

. . .and your own classroom . . .

Here lies the rub. Do everything you can to shift the work load to the kids. They are the ones who need to do the work. It is by doing things that students best learn—by taking risks, making mistakes, grappling with the material, pondering the questions, comparing and contrasting, analyzing the facts, reflecting on the information, talking it over with peers, questioning conclusions, responding without fear, doubting implausible answers, discarding unreliable information, raising uncertainties, surfacing tentative conclusions, acknowledging each other's contributions . . .and doing all of this in ways that allow them to take advantage of their own strengths and learning styles.

Observation Notes

Appendix B

Elementary/Middle School Language Arts Lesson Plan (45–55 minutes)

(Developed by Kathy Galford)

Unit: Elements of Poetry and Literature/Standardized Testing Review

Lesson: Figurative Language Review

I. Lesson Objectives

By the end of the lesson, students will:

a. recall and define the following figures of speech: simile, metaphor, onomatopoeia, hyperbole, personification, idiom (other literary terms can be substituted);

b. identify and sort examples of figures of speech (listed above) in literature selections; and

c. interact with classmates to form cooperative groups, brainstorm ideas, and complete a task

II. Lesson Materials/Supplies

a. Class set of index cards (1 per student) with examples of figures of speech

b. Six large sheets of bulletin board paper in different colors, posted throughout the classroom

c. Sentence strip labels for each of the figures of speech

d. Six poster boards or large pieces of construction paper divided into six sections and labeled with the six figures of speech

e. Markers

f. Six sets of index cards with examples of figures of speech taken from a literature selection previously read in class, such as a novel, short story, or poem

g. Class copies of graffiti game grid

h. Music player with selected songs

III. Lesson Procedure/Content

a. Teacher has volunteers distribute index cards with examples of figures of speech to their classmates. Each student should receive one card, and an equal number of the six figures of speech should be used. Teacher explains that the students will interact with their classmates to discover the topic of the review lesson.

b. While upbeat music plays, students circulate around the room, trading cards. Each time the music stops (2–3 times), they discuss the cards and what they have in common (adapted from Beth Estill's *Trade, Trade, Chat* activity).

c. Teacher prompts students to identify the topic of the lesson: figures of speech. Students are then instructed to find other classmates with the same figure of speech and stand with those students beside one of the large pieces of bulletin board paper.

d. Each group is asked to name the figure of speech their cards have in common. Corresponding sentence strip labels are placed at the top of each poster, and groups use markers to create a *Graffiti Wall* about their figure of speech, listing definitions, examples, and descriptions. Each time the music stops, groups rotate to other posters, reading the "graffiti" and adding to it.

e. When groups have rotated to each poster, teacher uses information on posters to lead a discussion of the six figures of speech.

    i. Simile: compares two things using *like* or *as*

    ii. Metaphor: compares two things as if one thing is or becomes another

    iii. Hyperbole: extreme exaggeration

    iv. Onomatopoeia: words that create sounds

    v. Personification: giving human traits to nonhuman things

    vi. Idiom: a phrase that means something other than the literal meaning of the words

f. Card sort activity: Teacher gives each group a set of cards with examples of figurative language taken from a literature selection previously read in class and a poster with sections for each of the six figures of speech. Students read the cards, discuss their meaning in the literature selection, and sort them according to the figure of speech as teacher circulates the room providing assistance and checking for understanding.

IV. Lesson Evaluation/Closing Activity

Graffiti Game:

a. Students are given a grid with squares containing definitions or examples of the figures of speech.

b. As music plays, students circulate throughout the room, finding classmates to write answers and their initials in the different squares on the grid. Only one student should write in each square. The first five students to turn in a completed grid win a small prize.

V. Extension Activities

a. Play songs containing figures of speech and pass out copies of lyrics to students. In groups, students highlight and discuss the figures of speech.

b. Students create their own songs, poems, or stories containing figures of speech.

c. Students write examples of figures of speech on Post-It notes and place them on the front chalkboard. During music, students take Post-Its off the front chalkboard and place them around the room on posters labeled with each figure of speech.

References

Allen, R. (2002). *Impact teaching: Ideas and strategies for teachers to maximize student learning*. Boston: Allyn & Bacon.

Allen, R. (2008). *Train smart: Effective trainings every time*. Thousand Oaks, CA: Corwin Press.

Armstrong, T. (2006). *The best schools: How human development research should inform educational practice*. Alexandria, VA: ASCD.

Bailey, B. (2001). *Conscious discipline: 7 basic skills for brain smart classroom management*. Oviedo, FL: Loving Guidance, Inc.

Bissel, B. (1992, July). *The paradoxical leader*. Paper presented at the Missouri Leadership Academy, Columbia, MO.

Blaydes Madigan, J. (2004). *Thinking on your feet* (2nd ed.). Murphy, TX: Action Based Learning.

Bluestein, J. (1999). *21st century discipline: Teaching students responsibility and self-management*. Torrance, CA: Fearon Teacher Aids.

Bluestein, J. (2001). *Creating emotionally safe schools: A guide for educators and parents*. Deerfield Beach, FL: Health Communications, Inc.

Borja, R. (2005, November). TV in the bedroom a childhood norm. *Education Week, 25*(12), 11.

Bosch, K. (2006). *Planning classroom management: A five-step process to creating a positive learning environment* (2nd ed.). Thousand Oaks, CA: Corwin Press.

Bowman, D. (1998). *Presentations: Proven techniques for creating presentations that get results*. Holbrook, MA: Adams Media Corporation.

Boynton, B., & Boynton, C. (2005). *The educator's guide to preventing and solving discipline problems*. Alexandria, VA: ASCD.

Bracey, G. (2006, December). Students do NOT need high-level skills in today's job market. *The Education Digest, 72*(4), 24–28.

Brooks, J., & Brooks, M. (1999). *In search of understanding: The case for constructivist classrooms*. Alexandria, VA: ASCD.

Burke, K. (2008). *What to do with the kid who . . . Developing cooperation, self-discipline, and responsibility in the classroom* (3rd ed.). Thousand Oaks, CA: Corwin Press.

Burke, K. (2005). *How to assess authentic learning* (4th ed.). Thousand Oaks, CA: Corwin Press.

Burke, K. (2006). *From standards to rubrics in six steps: Tools for assessing student learning, K–8*. Thousand Oaks, CA: Corwin Press.

Conzemius, A., & O'Neill, J. (2006). *The power of smart goals: Using goals to improve student learning.* Bloomington, IN: Solution Tree.

Costa, A. (2000). Describing the habits of mind. In A. Costa & B. Kallick (Eds.), *Discovering & exploring habits of mind.* (pp. 21–40). Alexandria, VA: ASCD.

Costa, A. (2008). *The school as a home for the mind: Creating mindful curriculum, instruction, and dialogue.* Thousand Oaks, CA: Corwin Press.

Cramer, K. (2001, January). Using models to build an understanding of functions. *Mathematics Teaching in the Middle School,* National Council of Teachers of Mathematics, 6(5), 310–318.

Curwin, R. (2003). *Making good choices: Developing responsibility, respect, and self-discipline in Grades 4–9.* Thousand Oaks, CA: Corwin Press.

Danielson, C. (2002). *Enhancing student achievement: A framework for school improvement.* Alexandria, VA: ASCD.

Deming, W. E. (2000). *Out of the crisis.* Cambridge, MA: The MIT Press.

Dennison, P., & Dennison, G. (1994). *Brain gym(r) teacher's edition revised.* Ventura, CA: Edu-Kinesthetics.

Dickinson, D. (1995). Multiple technologies for multiple intelligences. In R. Fogarty & J. Bellanca (Eds.). *Multiple intelligences: A collection.* Arlington Heights, IL: IRI/Skylight Training and Publishing, Inc.

Di Giulio, R. C. (2007). *Positive classroom management: A step-by-step guide to helping students succeed.* Thousand Oaks, CA: Corwin Press.

Done, P. (2006, April). MAKE 'EM LAUGH (& THEY'LL LEARN A LOT MORE). *Instructor* (1999), 115(7), 32, 34–35.

Dunn, R., and Dunn, K. (2005) Thirty-five years of research on perceptual strengths: Essential strategies to promote learning. *The Clearing House,* 78(6), 273–276.

Erlauer, L. (2003). *The Brain-compatible classroom: Using what we know about learning to improve teaching.* Alexandria, VA: ASCD.

F de Wet, C. (2006, October). Beyond presentations: Using PowerPoint as an effective instructional tool. *Gifted Child Today,* 29(4), 29–39.

Feinstein, S. (2004). *Secrets of the teenage brain: Research-based strategies for reaching & teaching today's adolescents.* Thousand Oaks, CA: Corwin Press.

Fisher, D. & Frey, N. (2007). *Checking for understanding: Formative assessment techniques for your classroom.* Alexandria, VA: ASCD.

Fogarty, R. (1990). *Designs for cooperative interactions.* Thousand Oaks, CA: Corwin Press.

Fogarty, R., & Bellanca, J. (1995). *Multiple intelligences: A collection.* IRI/Skylight Training and Publishing, Inc.

Garmston, R. (1997). *The presenter's fieldbook: A practical guide.* Norwood, MA: Christopher Gordon Publishers.

Garmston, R., & Wellman, B. (1992). *How to make presentations that teach and transform.* Alexandria, VA: ASCD.

Garmston, R., & Wellman, B. (1999). *The adaptive school: A sourcebook for developing collaborative groups.* Norwood, MA: Christopher Gordon Publishers.

Gewertz, C. (2007, June). Diplomas count: Ready for what? Preparing students for college, careers, and life after high school. *Education Week,* 26(40), 25–27.

Glazer, S. (2006, August). A good icebreaker. *Teaching Pre K–8, 37*(1), 86–87.

Goodlad, J. (2004). *A place called school* (2nd ed.). New York: McGraw-Hill.

Gordon, G. (2006). *Building engaged schools: Getting the most out of America's classrooms.* New York: Gallup Press.

Green, J. (2002). *The green book of songs by subject—A thematic guide to popular music* (5th ed.). Nashville, TN: Professional Desk Reference.

Gregory, G. (2005). *Differentiating instruction with style: Aligning teacher and learner intelligences for maximum achievement.* Thousand Oaks, CA: Corwin Press.

Gregory, G. & Chapman, C. (2002). *Differentiated instructional strategies: One size doesn't fit all.* Thousand Oaks, CA: Corwin Press.

Grinder, M. (2000). *A healthy classroom.* Battle Ground, WA: Michael Grinder & Associates.

Hannaford, C. (2005). *Smart moves: Why learning is not all in your head* (2nd ed.). Salt Lake City, UT: Great River Books.

Hoff, R. (1992). *"I can see you naked."* Kansas City: Andrews and McMeel.

Jenkins, L. (2003). *Improving student learning: Applying Deming's quality principles in classrooms* (2nd ed.). Milwaukee, WI: ASQ Quality Press.

Jenkins, L. (2005). *Permission to forget: And nine other root causes of America's frustration with education.* Milwaukee, WI: ASQ Quality Press.

Jensen, E. (1998). *Trainer's bonanza: Over 1000 fabulous tips & tools.* San Diego, CA: The Brain Store, Inc.

Jensen, E. (2000a). *Learning with the body in mind.* Thousand Oaks, CA: Corwin Press.

Jensen, E. (2000b). *Music with the brain in mind.* San Diego, CA: The Brain Store.

Jensen, E. (2005a). *Teaching with the brain in mind* (2nd ed.). Alexandria, VA: ASCD.

Jensen, E. (2005b). *Top tunes for teaching: 977 song titles & practical tools for choosing the right music every time.* San Diego, CA: The Brain Store.

Jensen, E. (2007). *Introduction to brain-compatible learning* (2nd ed.). Thousand Oaks, CA: Corwin Press.

Jones, F. (2007). *Tools for teaching* (2nd ed.). Santa Cruz, CA: Fredric H. Jones & Associates, Inc.

Kagan, S. (1994). *Cooperative learning.* San Clemente, CA: Kagan Cooperative Learning.

Kaufeldt, M. (2005). *Teachers, change your bait! Brain-compatible differentiated instruction.* Bethel, CT: Crown House Publishing.

Knight, J. (2007). *Instructional coaching: A partnership approach to improving instruction.* Thousand Oaks, CA: Corwin Press and NSDC.

Kohn, A. (1999). *The schools our children deserve.* New York: Houghton Mifflin.

Koutoufas, L. (2007). Lessons from the second year: What I learned from the first grade. In P. Bigler & S. Bishop (Eds.), *Be a teacher—You can make a difference—By America's finest teachers.* (pp. 106–121). St. Petersburg, FL: Vandamere Press.

Lezotte, L. (1992). *Creating the total quality effective school.* Okemos, MI: Effective Schools Products, Ltd.

Lipman, D. (1999). *Improving your storytelling: Beyond the basics for all who tell stories in work or play.* Atlanta, GA: August House Publishers, Inc.

Lipton, L., and Wellman, B. (2000). *Pathways to understanding: Patterns and practices in the learning-focused classroom* (3rd ed.). Guilford, VT: Pathways Publishing.

Lipton, L., and Wellman, B. (2001). *Mentoring matters: A practical guide to learning-focused relationships.* Sherman, CT: MiraVia LLC.

Maguire, J. (1998). *The power of personal storytelling: Spinning tales to connect with others.* New York: Jeremy P. Tarcher/Putnam.

Marzano, R. (2007). *The art and science of teaching: A comprehensive framework for effective instruction.* Alexandria, VA: ASCD.

Marzano, R. (2003). *What works in schools: Translating research into action.* Alexandria, VA: ASCD.

Nathanson, S. (2006). Harnessing the power of story: Using narrative reading and writing across content areas. *Reading Horizons, 47*(1), 1–26.

Nelson, B. (1996). Cooperative learning. *The Science Teacher, 63*(5), 22–25.

Ollerenshaw, J., & Lowery, R. (2006). Storytelling: Eight steps that help you engage your students. *Voices From the Middle, 14*(1), 30–31, 34–37.

Parry, T., & Gregory, G. (1998). *Designing brain-compatible learning.* Arlington Heights, IL: Skylight Professional Development.

Rogers, S., & Renard, L. (1999, September). Relationship-driven teaching. *Educational Leadership, 57*(1), 34–37

Rowe, M. (1986). Wait time: Slowing down may be a way of speeding up! *Journal of Teacher Education, 37*(1), 43–50.

Searson, R., and Dunn, R. (2001). The learning-style teaching model. *Science and Children, 38*(5): 22–26.

Smith, R. (2004). *Conscious classroom management: Unlocking the secrets of great teaching.* Fairfax, CA: Conscious Teaching Publications.

Sousa, D. (2001). *How the brain learns.* Thousand Oaks, CA: Corwin Press.

Sprenger, M. (2002). *Becoming a "wiz" at brain-based teaching.* Thousand Oaks, CA: Corwin Press.

Sylwester, R. (1995). *A celebration of neurons: An educator's guide to the human brain.* Alexandria, VA: ASCD.

Tate, M. (2003). *Worksheets won't grow dendrites.* Thousand Oaks, CA: Corwin Press.

Tate, M. (2007). *Shouting won't grow dendrites.* Thousand Oaks, CA: Corwin Press.

Tileston, D. W. (2004). *What every teacher should know about student motivation.* Thousand Oaks, CA: Corwin Press.

Tomlinson, C., & McTighe, J. (2006). *Integrating differentiated instruction & understanding by design: Connecting content and kids.* Alexandria, VA: ASCD.

Whitaker, T. (2004). *What great teachers do differently: 14 things that matter most.* Larchmont, NY: Eye on Education.

White, Michael. (2000). *Leonardo: The first scientist.* New York: St. Martin' Press.

Wicks, C., Peregoy, J., & Wheeler, J. (2001). *Plugged in! A teacher's handbook for using total quality tools to help kids conquer the curriculum.* New Bern, NC: Class Action.

Wolfe, P. (2001). *Brain matters: Translating research into classroom practice.* Alexandria, VA: ASCD.

Wong, H., & Wong, R. (2005). *How to be an effective teacher: The first days of school*. Mountain View, CA: Harry K. Wong Publications, Inc.

Wubbels, T., Levy, J., & Brekelmans, M. (1997, April). Paying attention to relationships. *Educational Leadership, 54*(7), 82–86.

Index

CORWIN PRESS

The Corwin Press logo—a raven striding across an open book—represents the union of courage and learning. Corwin Press is committed to improving education for all learners by publishing books and other professional development resources for those serving the field of PreK–12 education. By providing practical, hands-on materials, Corwin Press continues to carry out the promise of its motto: **"Helping Educators Do Their Work Better."**